PRAISE FOR *EVERBLOOM*

"Once I began reading these stories I couldn't stop. Each writer is a strong woman who has learned much from life and God. Gritty, funny, painful, affirming. No punches are pulled, but grace abounds."

—LUCI SHAW, poet, author of *Thumbprint in the Clay*

"Readers will find gold within these pages. Excellent writing often springs from deep sorrow that has softened hearts, widened vision, and presses its bearer into the Man of Sorrows."

—DEE BRESTIN, author of *The Friendships of Women*

"We read to see elements of our own hearts, experiences and stories reflected back to us in the words of others. This collection is just that: stories that help us feel seen, known, and understood. Honestly and beautifully told, this book will keep you in good company along your own journey."

—SHAUNA NIEQUIST, bestselling author of *Present Over Perfect*

"*Everbloom* isn't just a book... it's a collection of stories that inspire courage, promote honesty, and promise freedom. When you travel through the journeys of these amazing women, don't be surprised if you discover hope for your own story."

—CALEB KALTENBACH, Lead Pastor, Discovery Church,
author of *Messy Grace* and *God of Tomorrow*

"*Everbloom* contains a smorgasbord of personal stories and reflections that put the strong writing of women and the reality of women's lives on display. I suspect every reader will find themselves in one or more of these chapters. But beyond giving readers a lot to ponder, these writers are also offering readers with a story to tell the kind of support they've been offering each other. Each chapter contains a "you can do it too" Writing Prompt to inspire the reluctant writer to get started."

—CAROLYN CUSTIS JAMES,
author of *Half the Church: Recapturing God's Global Vision for Women* and
Malestrom: Manhood Swept into the Currents of a Changing World

Ever
BLOOM

STORIES *of* LIVING DEEPLY ROOTED
AND TRANSFORMED LIVES

by women of
Redbud
WRITERS GUILD

**Edited by Shayne Moore
and Margaret Ann Philbrick**

PARACLETE PRESS
BREWSTER, MASSACHUSETTS

2017 First Printing

Everbloom: Stories of Living Deeply Rooted and Transformed Lives

Copyright © 2017 by Redbud Writers Guild

ISBN 978-1-61261-933-0

"Silent Sentinel" by Emily Gibson was previously published in *Root Exposure: New Voices in Literature* by Stephanie Rogers (Author, Editor), Andrew Abang, Harmoni McGlothlin (Editors), CreateSpace Independent Publishing Platform, 2009.

"Caretakers of the World" by Shayne Moore was previously published in *Global Soccer Mom: Changing the World Is Easier Than You Think*. Grand Rapids, MI: Zondervan, 2011; 18–27.

The Paraclete Press name and logo (dove on cross) are trademarks of Paraclete Press, Inc.

Library of Congress Cataloging-in-Publication Data

Names: Redbud Writers Guild. | Moore, Shayne, 1970- compiler.
Title: Everbloom : stories of living deeply rooted and transformed lives / by
   the women of Redbud Writers Guild ; compiled by Shayne Moore And Margaret
   Ann Philbrick.
Description: Brewster MA : Paraclete Press Inc., 2017. | Includes
   bibliographical references.
Identifiers: LCCN 2016057855 | ISBN 9781612619330 (trade paper)
Subjects: LCSH: Christian women--Religious life. | Christian biography.
Classification: LCC BV4527 .R4245 2017 | DDC 248.8/43--dc23
LC record available at https://lccn.loc.gov/2016057855

10 9 8 7 6 5 4 3 2 1

Published by Paraclete Press
Brewster, Massachusetts
www.paracletepress.com
Printed in the United States of America

Dedicated to all women who have yet to find freedom in Christ in order to embrace their story and share it with the world. We believe in you, and we pray this book will help you "walk right up to him and get what he is so ready to give. Take the mercy, accept the help." (Heb. 4:16 MSG)

And then the day came,
when the risk
to remain tight
in a bud
was more painful
than the risk
it took
to Blossom.

—ANAÏS NIN

TABLE *of* CONTENTS

Branches

Blossoms

Stephen King explains in his acclaimed bestseller *On Writing: A Memoir of the Craft*, "Honesty [in writing] makes up for a great many faults . . . but lying is the great unrepairable fault. Liars prosper, no question about it, but only in the grand sweep of things, never down in the jungles of actual composition, where you must take your objective one bloody word at a time. If you begin to lie about what you know and feel while you're down there, everything falls apart."

The distinctive culture of Redbud Writers Guild is our sense of community and our noncompetitive support for one another. Redbud was born out of a small group of women sharing the writing experience. Since the beginning, members have met together regularly. It is a safe place to create, to take risks, and to be honest.

Redbud has grown to include women from all over the world with a vision and a mission to fearlessly expand the feminine voice in our communities, faith, and culture. More often than not, our meetings now happen on social media and monthly mentoring video calls. Our community overflows with generosity toward one another and support for each other as we live into our Christian faith and our calling and vocation as writers.

Honesty is the heart of every good and true story. Connecting with a group of safe journey-women is a game changer. Many of us can testify to this truth. How many books, proposals, articles, and inspirations have been born in Redbud? Sitting together sipping wine or coffee, eating chocolate and warm apple crisp, even staring at a computer screen—community brings our writing off the page and into the here and now and into relationship.

And it keeps us honest. To have wise and discerning readers thoughtfully digesting newborn ideas can seem intimidating until you are blessed to go through the loving process. It keeps us honest, emotionally and spiritually, to see and hear how readers receive what we have written. We are challenged in the places where we can go deeper or need more clarity, and in the places we ought to cut altogether.

In these pages, we hope you see our honesty, and we invite you to join your story together with ours. At the end of each selection, you will find a writing or journaling prompt and a prayer to assist you.

May you be blessed by our stories as you find your own.

Shayne Moore,
Founder, Redbud Writers Guild, NFP
Margaret Ann Philbrick,
Redbud Board of Directors

We Write
by Margaret Ann Philbrick

We write
when fear rattles
our two a.m. feedings,
menopause flashes,
and our just lost his third job husband
rolls over again.

We crawl
down laundry strewn stairs
to set keys clicking
our kitchen table hopes
for healing, wholeness,
the end of terror.

We believe
in the singularity of our coffee mugs as
companions to
sermons, essays, proposals
composed alone, but
shared and shredded
as sisters.

We write
through cancer,
deadbeat fathers,
bipolar daughters,
dementia mothers,
and if He gives
a deep water immersion
of courage, our secrets.

We tuck
in cafe corners,
town libraries,
California wine bars,
numb and broken
because even Yeats
dulled the pain.

We listen
for a whisper
in the falling Redbud blossom speaking,
SLOW DOWN,
breathe, sing, see.

We envy
the unattainable,
the Proverbs 31 woman
and we try,
yes, we try to
climb Kilimanjaro,
crush HIV,
dance out urban decay,
set a table,

catch a fish,
and feed them.
Oh, we feed them,
words.
Every word,
we write,
for Him.

■ PRAYER

Heavenly Father, thank you for making yours the great story. Thank you for being the crafter of our stories and the feeder of our souls. I entrust mine to you. Lord, please reveal how the story you are calling me to tell reflects your gracious gifts and life. I ask for sacred space, time, and patience to receive your good gifts and share them with the world. Amen.

■ WRITING PROMPT

Describe an experience of feeding others.

Roots

The Woman Under the Palm Tree
by Jenny Rae Armstrong

I was nine years old when it happened, peering out the window of our second-story apartment in Monrovia, Liberia. The multiplex we lived in was in a good area, popular with internationals; the families on the top story were from India, the Peace Corps volunteers across the hall were American like us, and Mrs. Richards, the Liberian woman who owned the place, claimed the bottom level for her sprawling family, which seemed to be made up entirely of women and children. It was right across the street from JFK Hospital (ominously dubbed the "just for killing" hospital by the locals), where Mrs. Richard's live-in nieces, nephews, grandchildren, and I took turns donning my Care Bear roller skates and zipping down the cracked concrete wheelchair ramps, launching ourselves into the foliage that had muscled its way up through the pavement. We had a coconut tree in the front yard, a persimmon tree in the back, and a high concrete wall separating the clean, well-kept courtyard from the neglected street.

But if you looked out our hallway window, you could see the part of town where people lived in zinc shacks and cooked their meals on "country stoves," camp-style burners with an open flame for boiling rice and frying plantain. It wasn't off-limits necessarily—I'd venture in that direction to buy peanut candy and sour green oranges from market ladies, and several kids from that neighborhood would come over to play four square and teach us Bassa cuss words—but it was not a place where we spent much time.

I was standing at that hallway window, gazing down at the scene unfolding just outside our wall. A woman was curled up on her side under a palm tree, worn T-shirt stretched thin across her torso as she shielded her head with her dusty black arms, lappa-clad knees tucked close to her chest. The man kicking her wore camouflage, and had a government-issued machine gun slung over his shoulder.

I was horrified.

It wasn't that I hadn't witnessed beatings before. I had. It wasn't unusual to see mothers beating their children for disobedience or mistakes, preparing them to survive in unforgiving circumstances. Cries of "Rogue! Rogue!" would ring through our neighborhood as mobs chased down petty thieves; my father would sprint out the door to try to stop the flogging sure to take place when the offender was caught. But this was different, an armed man beating a helpless, cringing woman. And I had heard the whispers, the muted conversations adults thought I was too young to understand, about what men with guns did to women.

I heard my father's footsteps approaching and stood as still as possible, expecting to be shooed away from the window. But he stopped a few steps behind me and just stood there, watching the scene over my head. Or maybe watching me watch the scene. Then he sighed, turned, and walked away without a word.

The tectonic plates of my young soul shifted. Why wasn't my father, my hero, going out there to help the woman? What was different between this and all other times when he had intervened?

Slowly and sure as sunrise, it dawned on me that the gun threw the weight of the government behind the man and the violence he was meting out. It occurred to me that since this was happening in broad daylight, the soldier was probably the woman's husband, her only source of economic support. Maybe she didn't have a mama like Mrs. Richards, a fierce and competent matriarch, to scare away the riffraff and shelter her when things turned sour. If my father charged out there and did what every fiber of his Midwestern upbringing was undoubtedly screaming at him to do, it would likely spur the man on to further violence, and make matters worse for the woman.

For the first time, I understood that there were some problems my father, the strong, white, influential American man, couldn't fix.

He couldn't fix it, because the scourge of violence against women is not a simple battle that a strong army can rush in and win. It is a pandemic, a highly contagious pathogen that eats away at the hearts, minds, and souls of men, women, and children. It is a noxious weed that spreads more spores when attacked with swinging machetes. Strategic intervention is necessary, but you can't just treat the symptoms or mow the weed down from the top. You need to go deep under the surface, identify the source of the disorder, and neutralize the violence where it begins, in the small seed of pride, disdain, bitterness, or despair dropped into the human heart.

But if a tiny seed could sprout into that pervasive ugliness, why couldn't a tiny seed of something better, something stronger, overtake it and choke it out? I had seen the native foliage break through concrete at the "just for killing" hospital, knew that tiny living organisms with interlocking root systems could decimate ugly gray structures that had stood for generations. Maybe this was not a job for warriors, for powerful men with worldly influence. Maybe this was a job for gardeners, for people with patience, persistence, and a steely commitment to making the world a more beautiful place, one soul at a time. A job for elderly grandmothers and outraged aunties, for concerned sisters and countercultural men—for little girls armed with nothing more than righteous indignation, a life to spend, and a willingness to put their hand to the plow.

I felt a seed of something better, something stronger, drop into my nine-year-old soul, and I patted the soil around my newly acquired resolve.

What shall we say the kingdom of God is like, or what parable
shall we use to describe it? It is like a mustard seed, which is the
smallest of all seeds on earth. Yet when planted, it grows and
becomes the largest of all garden plants, with such big branches
that the birds can perch in its shade.
—Mark 4:30b–32 (NIV)

■ PRAYER

Jesus, perfect Lamb of God, you know what it is to suffer the helplessness
and horror of violence. Strengthen me to stand against injustice; give
me wisdom and courage as I work for shalom. In your name I pray.
Amen.

■ WRITING PROMPT

Describe a time when you felt helpless in the face of injustice. What
did you or anyone around you do about it?

The Tamarisk
by Jen Pollock Michel

t was dismembered in a morning. Before I had returned from driving my children to school, the crew had assembled. They were severing limbs with alacrity when I arrived. Weeks earlier, when a city arborist had knocked on the front door, conveying they'd "need to take her down to the stump," I had nodded and feigned sadness. But the truth was: I had no attachment to the diseased tree. Three years in our Toronto rental home was not adequate time for loyalty or grief, not when the future would uproot our expatriate life. Indifference was one luxury of our impermanence.

But when the chainsaws were loosed unexpectedly on a gray October morning, my detachment was felled like timber. I was angry that no one had informed us of the scheduled surgery, saddened that no one had insisted on good-byes. When the hard-hatted men broke the tree's brittle skeleton, I thought in alarm of the picture my youngest daughter had hoped to take. "I want to remember what it looked like." Before we could devise proper burial rites, the tree was mulched.

In the final chapter of Wendell Berry's novel *Jayber Crow*, rapacious Troy Chatham razes the last grove of trees on his dead father-in-law's farmland. Having exhausted the land by his appetite for profit and growth, Troy tries staving off bankruptcy with the one remaining source of income: logs. "What did he have left?" Jayber, his neighbor, asks himself, outraged. "Another cutting of timber, maybe, if he could wait another hundred or two hundred years."[1] To Troy, the trees were merchandise—logs to be felled and hauled away and sold. To Jayber, the trees represented not trunks and branches to be bundled for market but the stability of generations. They were a community's self-recognition, landmarks by which one knew to find his way. Trees provided roots of memory driven deep in the soil of years.

I confess to having lived much of my life without roots. When I was a child, my family packed and unpacked life every three years in a new city, often a new state. Like other American families, we chased the tail of opportunity. My father had been a high-school teacher, then a graduate student. As soon as he finished his dissertation, we moved from Indiana to East Tennessee for his first professorship, marveling that Southern soil could be so ruddy. Several years later, we left the red clay and the fragrance of dogwoods for another teaching job. A promotion. But even then, we didn't stay. Because when my grandparents' health failed, our tours of duty ended and we moved home (if it can be called that) to Ohio, the place where my mother had spent her childhood.

It is easy to say that I regretted my family's transience: children fault their parents something. But if I lamented my geographic instability growing up, I didn't leave it behind, even after marrying a man born and raised in the same Chicago suburb, a man who knew how to stay put. Opportunity waned, and we moved. And moved again. Sometimes we moved for career; sometimes for the dim sense of a call. Usually it had felt right. Always it had seemed necessary. But now that we've lived in Toronto for five years and our bureaucratic paperwork has been renewed twice, I've begun to grieve the roots we have failed to plant. The children have grown tall and lean. And still— we have no permanent address.

I find it immensely hopeful that Abraham, the hero of our faith, might also have been called a wanderer. He was called by God, quite insistently, to leave Haran: "Go from your country and your kindred and your father's house" (Gen. 12:1 esv). Despite God's simultaneous promise of a new home, Abraham spent the remainder of his years wandering. His life replayed the same song, like a narrative needle catching a groove. Abraham pitched tents and pulled up stakes. At the time of his death, the only land Abraham owned was the cave of Machpelah, which he had purchased as Sarah's burial site. Even Abraham's nephew, Lot, managed more stability than he (that is, before brimstone and fire hailed on Sodom). While Abraham was a man of tents, the author of Genesis notes that Lot's house—a more permanent structure—had a roof beam (Gen. 19:8).

Genesis 12 records God's sure promise of land and family to Abraham. I'll give you roots, God said. But if we're honest, throughout the course of his life, Abraham endured constant threat of instability. Famine. An insecure water supply. His wife's barrenness. Most terribly, in haunting echo of chapter 12, God issued another tripartite command in Genesis 22: "Take your son, your only son Isaac, whom you love, and go" (Gen. 22:2 ESV). On his way to Mount Moriah, Abraham must have surely found himself wondering about the divine method. In this moment—and in others—God's promises loomed like a mirage on the horizon; they seemed to evaporate the moment he got near them.

The author of Hebrews examines the resilience of hope that Abraham exercised in Genesis 22—indeed, throughout his entire life. Like others who followed in his stead, Abraham came to believe that permanence could never be wrested from the land. Yes, by the sure grace of God, he was living the home-going story of the Gospel, but home wasn't about the dirt beneath his feet. In all that wandering, Abraham learned to desire a better country. From Haran to Canaan to Egypt and back, Abraham learned to follow a God who had prepared for him—and for all of God's children—a greater city. That future hope made it easier to risk, easier to lose, easier to trust. It even made possible the binding of his own son, his only son, the son of his greatest affection—the son of God's promise—on an altar.

In the rented life that is mine, I can only hope I am gaining something of Abraham's faith. The future stretches before me, and she slyly keeps her secrets. Where is home? Where will I be in five years?

Or twenty? For while my husband has recently been offered a position in Toronto that looks to afford us several more years in Canada, and we will even begin application for permanent residency, we do not assume guarantees. We do, however, begin seizing the invitation of the in-between places: find solid ground. There is greater permanence than a permanent address. Most importantly, we look to learn that the God of Abraham—not the land, not the son—is himself the reward (Gen. 15:1).

In an inconspicuous scene from Abraham's life, the patriarch seals a treaty with Abimelech and secures ownership of a well. That water symbolizes prosperity, permanence, provision. Beersheba, he calls the place—well of the oath (Gen. 21:31). To honor the promise-keeping God and his promise of home, Abraham plants a tree—a tamarisk. Different from the strong and sturdy oaks that Abraham first encounters upon his entrance to the land of promise—trees owned by the Canaanites—the tamarisk is the tree of the wanderer. As Bible scholars note, it is a tree often planted by the Bedouin for the purposes of shade and feeding the grazing animals. It survives with shallow roots in sandy soil.

When Abraham plants the tamarisk, he calls on the Lord, choosing a name that speaks permanence: Everlasting God. Nevertheless, the tale of the tamarisk doesn't conclude Abraham's journey, for Scripture records that "Abraham sojourned many days in the land of the Philistines" (Gen. 21:34 ESV). But it does remind us that for every wanderer, roots are possible in the stable soil of God.

■ PRAYER

Lord, help me to be content with your way of establishing home in my life. Sometimes it feels unstable, haphazard, a jigsaw road of twists and turns. At those times, turn my heart to your promise in John 14:23—

that you and the Father and the Holy Spirit will make your home in us. Root me in this truth, as my heart's home. Amen.

■ WRITING PROMPT

Where do you feel most rooted and at home?

Untangle
by Sarah Rennicke

ere I sit at the airport terminal, waiting to head back to Kansas City after a surprise weekend for my brother's birthday. It's been three years since I moved from Milwaukee, and you'd think I'd be used to the alternation of flights between home and where I now reside. I'm not. I have been uprooted and yanked from my soil—good soil I sat in for twenty-eight years—and transplanted to foreign terrain, unfamiliar bearings.

Passengers spill into the terminal, men and women looking tired and content to arrive. I am mentally imploring the plane to unload forever so I will not have to board.

I am too familiar with airports, hum of engines, whir of thoughts. Constant middle ground—it's no longer where I grew comfortable; I have difficulty gaining my footing in the new. I cannot stop fidgeting under God's hands, though I realize he's trying to work in me.

Daily life moves on, and they call my group to board. I shuffle down the aisle and hide in the back, next to the oval window that will let me glimpse Lake Michigan until we rise above the clouds. With lift of metal wings, I am air bound, suspended between lands. Root-detaching again and again as I split time in two places.

I had thought I would spend my entire life in my Wisconsin hometown. Even if my ministry took me traveling, I would always return from my rounds to the curved streets I know so well. Or, at the very least, I'd stay within the state. Within driving distance to get to my family. I had wound my roots deep and did not want to uncurl them for anything.

Then, in a whirlwind I never saw coming, I was stripped of familiarity, wrenched from the warmth and love I reveled in, and planted where I was the new girl, with a job I wouldn't necessarily pick for myself. The span of time from application to acceptance was three weeks, and I moved to Kansas City two and a half weeks later. Knowing no one. But they needed me there as soon as possible, and I, in faith—or naively, as I see it now—took the leap and landed nine hundred miles away from the world I loved. For the sake of my growth, my gut assured me—for the calling of God.

I thrive on community and closeness, coming from a small town where I'm bound to run into someone I know whenever I go out. I landed in the second largest city in the state with overbearing traffic, people, and buildings. Nothing was like home; I was utterly alone in body and spirit. Though many gracious people went out of their way to make me feel welcome, no one could understand the loneliness, the unsettling that I could not seem to shake. I wandered grocery aisles, staring in a haze at all the cereal offerings while resigning to the truth that not a single face around would recognize mine. Wave after wave of struggle crashed over me: physical unfamiliarity, feeling lost, an emotional dismembering that left me gutted, and a spiritual barrenness that broke me down to levels deeper than I knew existed in me. My roots strained to find firm holding. And in the winds thrashing and threatening to break me open, plenty of questions sprang up in the tossed-about upheaval of faith.

How can a nurturing God pull me from where I am happy and have purpose, only to shove me into hard, barren ground with no belonging?

What if I never again feel settled and live a nomad's life, unable to acclimate, always out of place?

How long can I simply survive when I long to thrive?

Will I wander like the Israelites for forty years too long because of my grumbling?

What happens when I cannot feel the ground beneath my feet? When all I have is the unseen?

Too much. It is all too much.

Below me, patches of green and brown blend together along rivers as cracks in pavement. The world looks so ordered from a great distance. At eye level, everything is jumbled. When I'm stuck in the air, flux of fear and fierceness embrace this discomfort. Keep me flying. Let me stay thousands of feet in the air, and I won't have to walk back into what's waiting for me when I land.

People ask if I see myself living in Kansas City for a long time. What is long? These last few years have been an eternity, and I'm still spinning. I am expected to give my ten-year plan—but all I have is now. This is not my life plan; this is my here. It's been long enough where people expect me to be transitioned and settled, forming my life with joy and abundance. But I still miss the calm of the lake, the bend of road I can reach without thinking, the gentle assurance of my family's unending love and constant belief in me. I still struggle to belong—anchor my limbs and dig deep in the dregs of faith for belief that God is good and he is for me. That it is his hands that reach to release me from the fowler's snare that I might come into new life, one small sprout at a time. But first begins acceptance of a life never imagined, slowly becoming.

This cultivation has not felt good. But a good God is at work getting his hands dirty. Faith must form on its own time, in my choosing—choosing to believe he will not leave me shivering, exposed. My choosing to tie my shifting soul to him.

Light dances across the aisle while the stewardess passes cups of orange juice, coffee with steam that ribbons from the rim. Early morning rays stream through the glass, absorbed by strangers. I am not alone. We are all going somewhere, on some adventure, smack dab in the middle of this moment.

Maybe it's not necessarily the place but the promise: That I will see God's goodness in the land of the living—even when the expanse is barren space, he will yet restore my life, the hope of my salvation. That he is loving to me—because I am his daughter and he takes care where I am planted.

You can do this, I tell myself as my mind smooths out along the sky. I write the words with blue ink across the lines of my journal like a covenant. *Untangle your clenched fists which refuse God his turn at cultivating your heart.* I can replant and let God grow me in the life I never imagined. Let him loosen what I've clutched too tight.

The hardest season is this wait. Where there is no produce, no gain—just guts and guesses and tears watering the ground. The thing about planting is patience. It takes time for terrific things to bloom. Though I may second-guess and kick against the restraint, I find there's even more room for me to spread and get comfortable. Maybe I am ready to relearn that my heart is more adaptable than I thought. That it can stretch, tear, and still stand after all the strain.

Tires squeal smoke across the tarmac. Pieces of my growing-up life scatter behind the tail of the plane as we roll to our gate. Gathering my journal back up in my bag, I survey the seats around me. Inhale stale air into my nostrils. It all begins again at this point. Here we go. Breath pushed out of lungs. Submerge back into the soil of this rickety season. Accept the line of life I'm in, and give to God the planting trowel. Smile through the sting, linger in his love, and allow him to unfurl my knotted heart full of fear from this unknown. And maybe—could it be possible?—shift my perspective to anticipate what he will bring to blossom.

Following Jesus requires my all, not pieces scattered here and there, given and then taken away because it doesn't feel right. He calls for complete devotion, but allows the freedom of struggle as I mourn what I have given up in the process. For me, it was familiarity, belonging, and the way I laid out my days. But of course, the best way to push up from the ground is to lay down my life, hand him my heart, and have trust that he will settle me where it will be for his glory and my gain.

I set foot in Kansas City and scents of barbeque, espresso, and independence assail me as I make my way to the baggage claim. Here is now, and here is him. Remember. Release. Tonight I'll unpack my suitcase and summon up the courage to stay. For one more week. For more of him. For the chance that all of a sudden I'll wake to find I'm woven into this place, and the world around me will feel more like it's meant to—that where once there was only hardness, a sprig of hope softly nestles in to sprout and spread. I can be certain now that where my Christ resides, there is my home.

■ PRAYER

Father, my uprooting feels harsh and tender at the same time. I do not understand where you have taken me, or where we are going. I long to trust you to gently untangle the mess of my own stubbornness, living in limbo and refusing to anchor down. You see the full landscape. Please help me to dig in and allow my new roots to nestle in your care. Amen.

■ WRITING PROMPT

What has been painful but necessary for you to grow as a woman and in relationship with God?

Where I'm From
by *Nilwona Nowlin*

I am from the machete that cut sheet cakes *and* chopped weeds.
I am from Alaga syrup,
    lime green easy chairs
    and fried Spam and eggs on toast.
    I am from homemade jellies and jams,
    pineapple upside down cake,
    paella,
    hot water cornbread
    and "gov'ment" cheese.
The purple and gold Crown Royal bag filled with change
and the big gold covered Holy Bible that *leads* to change.
Hymns and Marvin Gaye.
House too full, house too loud.
I am from, "Girl, you slower than molasses in January!"
and "Yall don't believe fat meat greasy"
and "Yall be quiet in there, and go to sleep!"
The sizzle of the hot comb meeting thick hair,
"Hold your ear down."
"Ooo, girl, look at them kitchens!"
I am from doxologies
and decorating the fake Christmas tree.
Birthday cake and ice cream
and generic "puffa puffa wheat."
Dad's homemade egg nog
and Nat "King" Cole on the record player.
Roller skates and Funkytown.

I am from the mind of God,
   a precious child created in the Creator's image;
created to create.
   I am from hand-me-down clothes,
   handed out food
   and a handed down faith.
   "Sing a song full of the faith that the dark past has taught us.
   Sing a song full of the hope that the present has brought us.
   Facing the rising sun of a new day begun,
let us march on 'til victory is won!"

■ PRAYER

Heavenly Father, thank you for the wide spectrum of color that is your creation. Thank you for the smallest details that accompany my unique upbringing and story. Help me to embrace the unique images and associations of my life as a gift from you. Free me from a critical spirit when confronted by the unfamiliar aspects of someone else's life. Allow me to openly embrace differences when they make me uncomfortable, and may you receive the victory when I'm able. Amen.

■ WRITING PROMPT

Write a poem about how you hear God's voice of approval.

Finding Freedom from Fear
by Angie Ryg

I read it first on Facebook. Funny how something that was created to connect could make me feel so alone. This wasn't the loneliness of envy or the desire to be part of something. It was just the opposite—it was the wish to *not* be part of this story. I grew up with this story, and because of it. I am only now realizing how deep its tendrils of fear went into defining me. And there it was—a story you see on TV shows and milk cartons—a family's bittersweet resolution to over twenty-five years of pain. The country's mantra of "Jacob's Hope" came to the sad conclusion when a young boy's remains were finally found.

My second cousin, Jacob, was abducted from a small town in Minnesota. You begin to understand real fear when you hear how someone you know, someone you love, is taken by violence—and the worst part is you know nothing of the pain and evil. That became the biggest fear—not knowing the story. Every story has a beginning, middle, and end. The problem was, for most of my life, this story only had a beginning.

All over the news, the story was shared. The town was home to people who rarely locked their cars or homes, much less worried about the safety of taking a bike ride with friends. It happened at dusk, on a gravel road by an open field. "They" say there is safety in numbers. Where were "they" when a man came up and told the boys to get off their bikes? No one tells us in a group of three, one can get taken while two go free. They say not to talk to strangers, but they never say that if a stranger approaches you with a gun, you are better off running away even if he says he will not hurt you if you listen to him.

The news reports showed the field where it happened, the people walking the trails with candles lit with hope. They didn't show the call that traveled from Minnesota to a family in Illinois where a young girl heard that her second cousin had been taken. They didn't tell of this little girl's nightmares, thinking the same thing would happen to her.

The updates showed the face of Jacob displayed on buttons that read, "Jacob's Hope." They didn't show how this little girl would see the buttons at family reunions and be reminded the family was not complete.

Those buttons still haunt me.

People say our world changed on September 11, 2001, because people suddenly knew they were not safe. I grew up knowing this fear. It followed me into motherhood, my beautiful firstborn daughter, Leah, hearing, "You stay by me or you will get taken," on every outing. I minored in psychology, yet it wasn't until years later I would understand the power of fearful words. What I was saying planted seeds of distrust and robbed her little heart of the oblivious joy that she should feel at that young age.

Her little heart took in my truth, and it became twisted in her soul. Isn't that just what the Enemy does? Just like he twisted God's words in the Garden: "Did God really say you couldn't eat from any tree in the garden?" Satan hissed to Eve. And right then and there, Eve should have called on God to instruct, inspire, and prove Satan wrong!

I wanted her to know I was there for her, and she really was safe with us. *I wanted her to know no fear.* Instead, just like me, my little girl believed she would never be safe.

Years went by with three more children—blessings of beautiful life given to us by the Creator. Having seen Leah worry, I resolved to change how I approached my fear in parenting. I was not going to let fear win. With each child, I let them explore more, be more trusting, but I found I could not do it alone. I needed to weed out the seeds of fear and plant new seeds of hope.

God says that if we are tormented by fear, "this shows that we have not fully experienced his perfect love" (1 John 4:18b NLT). That made me really stop and think. When fear rises up, it should be a warning that we need to continue deepening our relationship with God.

> *There is no fear in love,*
> *but perfect love casts out fear.*
> —1 John 4:18a (ESV)

God says that perfect love drives out fear. But where do you find perfect love? If you look for perfect love in other people or circumstances, you will only be disappointed. The only way to experience perfect love is in an intimate relationship with your Heavenly Father. As I developed that intimate relationship with him, becoming more grounded in his perfect love, my fears became more unrealistic than my faith.

I needed God to help me with my fear of the unknown. I can relate to Sarah, Abraham's wife. Even as she was told she would have a child, I imagine the fear was overwhelming. Would her child be safe? What would he have to do in this life that God had chosen for him? What would he need to go through for her to be sanctified? I don't know about you, but those are the questions that would plague me. I would want control. I would struggle with fear of the unknown. I fear those things even now. Did Sarah's story turn out the way she had thought? Probably not. Trillia Newbell states the truth with such clarity:

Did [Sarah's story] turn out the way the Lord planned? Absolutely! And does God redeem it in the end? Yes. But you can't see the future in your own life like you get to in God's Word. We don't get the whole picture, do we? So we have to trust the Lord because only he knows. But there is one thing guaranteed, which is awaiting you all the days of your life: God's faithfulness.[2]

Just like Sarah, I have to trust the Lord because only he knows what each day holds in store for me or my family. Each story is a page in his book. The more I dig into God's Scriptures, the more I see how my life is not even really my story. It is his story, and it all leads back to the great story of redemption. My part in his great story is unknown, but I know he will finish the good work he began in us (Phil. 1:6). I must rest on the promise that he is our "Rock" and our "Redeemer" (Ps. 19:14).

God is "the author and finisher of our faith" (Heb. 12:2 KJV). *The author.* He already wrote my story. He already wrote yours. I know who holds the future in his hands, so when I read that the remains of Jacob had been found, there was no fear. The man who abducted Jacob showed the police where to find them. People may think his abductor wrote Jacob's story, but Jacob's story was written by God before the investigators had answers.

Jesus asks a poignant question in Matthew 6: "Which of you by being anxious can add a single hour to his span of life?" (Matt. 6:27 ESV). I can't. You can't. We need to remember God doesn't promise safety to his children, but he promises something even better: himself. He promises to never leave or forsake me (Deut. 31:6), and to give me strength and support: "So do not fear, for I am with you; do not be dismayed, for I am your God. I will strengthen you and help you; I will uphold you with my righteous right hand" (Isa. 41:10 NIV).

When I remain rooted in him and trust that he is sovereign in all circumstances, my faith is made stronger. By submersing myself in God's truth found in the Bible, I know God's faithfulness is far greater than my fear. This does not mean that my life will end up with a happily ever after. Jacob's story did not end up as we wanted. Prayers were not answered as we asked, but God is in control, and we must trust in his perfect plan. God is our Creator, Lord, Savior, and Judge. He is the one who has a plan for our lives that will bring him glory. Jacob's story is still very much filled with Hope—the Hope we have in Jesus.

Robby Gallaty shares in his book *Firmly Planted***,** "When Christ saved you, everything changed, including your way of thinking. Again, the word 'repentance,' which means changing one's direction, also involves adopting a new mindset—the mind of Christ (Phil. 2:5). Remember, belief drives behavior; a change of mind leads to a change of actions. When you begin to think like Jesus, you will soon begin to live like Jesus."[3] Christ's love transforms lives.

When I am grounded in God's love, I believe his promises and trust in his plan for my life. Only then can I find freedom from fear. Although there is evil in this world, God has overcome it. Living out this truth has allowed me to pass on a legacy of faith and joy to my children, who can find a freedom from fear and trust in God's perfect plan.

> *Give thanks to the* Lord*, for he is good.*
> *His love endures forever.*
> —Psalm 136:1 (NIV)

■ PRAYER

Dear Father, you are all-knowing. You are Love. You held the entire perfect plan for the world in your hands before any of us took our first breath. Instead of planting myself on the rock of my salvation, I often sway with the sin of fear and doubt. Forgive me. Help me desire more of you and your Word. Thank you for your faithfulness. Help me be joyful in hope, patient in affliction, and faithful in prayer so that my roots are deep in you and your glory may be shown. Amen.

■ WRITING PROMPT

What makes you afraid?

Moving Home
by Cara Meredith

Sometimes lament takes up permanent residence in our lives.

We'd finally found the perfect fit for our little family—a place where urban meets suburban in a lakeside neighborhood of Oakland, California. My husband and I relished the diverse culture around us, delighted that our young sons would grow up surrounded by people who looked like all of us. There would be folks with vanilla skin like Mama, and milk chocolate skin like Dada, and creamy caramel-colored skin, just like them.

"We struck gold!" we exclaimed to friends and family. "A real, live jackpot of a place! Designed just for us!" We wrote with exclamation points rampant in every sentence, after we gazed at the nearby elementary school the boys would attend someday soon.

We baked chocolate-chip oatmeal cookies, packaged them on cardboard plates, and dropped them off on the doorsteps of neighbors we'd known for only a couple of months. We visited Neighbor Paul's chickens almost daily, and we hung out in Lorenzo's driveway as he polished and shined his gold-rimmed 1972 El Camino. We dug into community, at our church and at the gym and at the Saturday morning farmers' market, because that's just what you do: you dig into the soil of people and relationships. You peel off the layers. You make them feel known, and in doing so, you realize that you, too, are just as much known and loved and understood.

In the meantime, you find yourself boldly proclaiming that you'll never leave. Surely, you'll grow old here. So, glory, glory, you raise all the flags heavenward, for you belong to this place and it belongs to you.

And, at least in my story, that's when lament enters the scene.

Because just when I think I'm in control, just when I've figured out where I'm going to settle down and let tangled roots grow deep, a brash uprooting occurs.

I pound my fist on the tabletop: This isn't what was supposed to happen. This isn't how it was supposed to happen. I was supposed to have time to say my good-byes. Even more so, I was supposed have a say in when I wanted to leave—and not only was our impending move not on my radar; it wasn't on the list of possibilities.

Neighbor Julie, who lives four doors past the chickens, knocks on my door. She's the kind of neighbor I always dreamed of, the type of person who piques a sense of curiosity within you, who wants to know you just as much as you want to know her. So, you have playdates together. You start a book club together. You go on hikes, and you gather your flocks under one roof when both of your husbands travel out of town. You find yourself knocking on one another's doors without a thought, because you can, because that's what you're supposed and allowed to do as neighbors.

Additionally, she's the kind of person I always hoped would rat-a-tat-tat on my front door, someone who would choose me just as much as I chose her.

"Oh friend," she says to me, and our bodies meet in hugging embrace.

She'd heard relocation was a possibility, but like me, she didn't actually think it'd happen—or at least not this fast. It was a really good idea on paper: a dream job in a company that values my husband just as much as he values working for them; a return to family and friends, to a people and land born in my blood; a place we can afford to live and settle down in with our young family, away from the skyrocketing costs of the Bay Area.

But sometimes, all the good reasons on paper still don't take away the ache.

We sit at opposite ends of the couch, cups of tea balancing on each of our laps. We stare not at each other but at the window in front of us, at the unknown, at the gray, at what feels like an inevitable end to us. Ours was a friendship born of convenience, strengthened by proximity and ease of access to one another's worlds.

"I'm really going to miss you, friend," she says to me, and my eyes fill with tears for the second time that morning.

"I'm really going to miss you, too."

Together, we cry. We cry over what has been, and we cry over what could have and would have been. We cry, because when we wrote the script, we naively had forever in mind. We cry because it's the end of an era—the end of a most idyllic, "how'd we get so lucky to land next to you" era. We cry because we don't know how this will end, and we cry because we know it won't be the same for us ever again.

Lament, I read, is telling God you're sad. Complaint, on the other hand, is being angry with God because you're sad. So, I ask of others, and of myself, can I be both? Am I allowed to sit in my living room with Neighbor Julie, and simultaneously be sorrow-filled and indignant, just for now?

Maybe it's a combination of the voices and the silence and the noises around me, or maybe it really is Spirit offering a truce to my soul, but I hear a gentle yes.

Yes, I see you. Yes, I hear you. Yes, I enter into your pain with you.

So, I let myself feel, because God himself lets me feel. When waves of lament and waves of complaint come, I thrash and I flail and I bump along accordingly. I don't run to the shore, as I am prone to do, but I ride the storm out. I gulp in mouthfuls of water. I spit out grains of sand. Then, when the intensity of grief is over, I float, I rest, I relish in peace.

I accept who we've become, at least for the time being: moving people. We're nomads. Itinerant wanderers. Reluctant pilgrims. Although we yearn to be rooted people—citizens whose roots dig deep into the earth, tangled in longevity and staying power, planted to stay in one place and never leave—that's not who we are, at least not for the time being. Instead, we're messy, dirt-laden, "pull us up by our stems and hope we survive the transplant" people.

But just as God gives me permission to feel all I need to feel, he gives me permission to transplant and to be transplanted, even if it's the last thing my heart wants to do.

And I don't doubt he does the same for you.

■ PRAYER

God, you see my tears. You hear my cries. You enter into my pain, and you stand with me. I stand on your promise that, when I mourn, you will be the Great Comforter—in that way, comfort me now so that I might see you in the ordinary everyday. Amen.

■ WRITING PROMPT

Describe a time when feelings of being transplanted left you with more tears than joy.

Finding Myself at Fenway
by Dorothy Greco

As a new believer, whenever I came across the story in John 5 about the paralytic, I was perplexed and annoyed by Jesus's question. Scripture tells us that the man, who had been sick for thirty-eight years, was lying on one of the porches hoping for someone to place him in the healing pool when the angel stirred the water. The apostle John writes, "When Jesus saw him lying there and learned that he had been in this condition for a long time, he asked him, 'Do you want to get well?'" (John 5:6 NIV). I would always respond on the paralytic's behalf, *Isn't that obvious?*

Ten years after I began my faith journey, Jesus asked me the same question.

The Setup

I joined more than a hundred writers, photographers, and TV crews all milling about Boston's Fenway Park in the hope of gathering pregame tidbits. The Red Sox were up against the Oakland A's for Game 1 of the American League East playoffs. The atmosphere was festive. Because I had been photographing professional sports for years in a city that deifies athletes, this scenario was familiar. My fragile emotions were not.

Less than forty-eight hours earlier, I had returned from an assignment in Romania—my final job after traversing the globe for two consecutive years. I had stayed with runaway teens under highway overpasses, witnessed bone-crushing poverty in the Dominican Republic, and come face-to-face with corrupt government officials in Central America. None of this prepared me for Romania.

Though the despotic leader, Nicolae Ceaușescu, had been executed, the results of his reign lingered. Grocery-store shelves were mostly empty except for dusty jars of pickled beets and sauerkraut. Electricity came on randomly for one or two hours a day. Industrial pollution blackened the sky. But the most devastating evidence of his evil regime was the orphanages.

Ceaușescu made birth control illegal. Simultaneously, he and his cronies skimmed the profits from the resource-rich country, plunging it into economic depression. Because many families could neither feed nor care for their children, they abandoned them to the state-run orphanages. These institutions were woefully understaffed and underresourced.

As soon as I stepped over the threshold of Romania's main orphanage, I started gagging at the smell of human waste. Cribs were crammed together, with only two narrow aisles bisecting the room. Ragged straps of cloth tethered many of the children to their bedframes to restrain them. More notable than the smell was the silence. In a room housing approximately two hundred children, the only sounds were barely audible moans. The combined effect of abandonment, neglect, and abuse left many of these orphans with listless bodies and vacant souls. After spending six hours in the center, I was completely and utterly undone.

Despite the five thousand miles between me and Romania, I could not forget what I had experienced. As I looked around Fenway, all I could see were the excesses of American life. Without warning, empathy and grief trumped self-control. I started weeping—while on the field—and couldn't stop. In a futile effort to compose myself, I retreated to the onsite photographer's darkroom and sobbed.

After a few moments, the editor banged on the door, wondering where his pregame photos were. I emerged, eyes bloodshot and red, and attempted to explain my highly unprofessional behavior. He responded, "You must have your period. If you can't pull it together, go home. I need someone who can get the job done." Understandable, if not *slightly* misogynistic. I did go home. That night was the beginning of the end of my sports photography career.

It was also the beginning of encountering God and becoming whole.

Stirring the Waters

One of my earliest memories is being criticized by my mother as being *too sensitive*. While playing in the sandbox my father had recently built for me and my sisters, I became increasingly agitated by the grittiness of the sand in my shoes. I repeatedly asked my mother to take off my little blue Keds, dump out the sand, and then retie them. This was pre-Velcro. Decades later, while parenting my own sensitive child, I suddenly understood her exasperation. And yet, these specific words, repeatedly uttered when my mother was frustrated by my neediness, created a fault line that ran from my head to my heart, leading me to conclude that I was irredeemably flawed.

Despite my longing to grow out of my sensitivities, they did not diminish. Line-dried sheets felt like knife blades against my skin at night. Smells overpowered me. Sudden loud noises sent my nervous system into overdrive. As the years went by, I did not become less sensitive—I simply learned how to hide my sensitivities and feign indifference. I honed my technique until I had the emotional EKG of a cadaver.

There was a high cost to this charade. To maintain this flat line, I had to be hypervigilant—always anticipating "what-ifs." And I had to be hypercontrolling. Though I had a rich network of friends, I was calculated in my vulnerability. I prided myself in never displaying anger or other negative emotions. And I certainly never cried in public. That was the ultimate taboo. So when I found myself weeping at the playoff game, I was mortified.

I could not see it in real time, but God's kingdom was breaking in. Just like the pool at Bethesda, healing waters were stirring. Circumstances converged, creating just enough inner turbulence to crack my load-bearing walls and cause my facades to crumple. It was both ugly and beautiful. In *The Broken Way*, Ann Voskamp writes, "If you didn't understand what life looks like, you might mistake it for complete destruction."[4] Indeed.

A long season of grief followed. I wept for the children in Romania. I wept for my father, broken in body and spirit from years of chemical addiction. I wept for my recently broken engagement and for those impacted by apartheid in South Africa. These tears allowed others to see my weaknesses and vulnerabilities. They also dissolved the cataracts that had prevented me from seeing God.

Like the blind man healed by Jesus who gains his sight incrementally (Mark 8), I slowly but surely began to see the Messiah as something more than a distant, historical figure. He became a constant friend, a protective brother, and a lover who recognized my sins but forgave them, even as he called me into greater wholeness. The fierceness of his love motivated and inspired me to do whatever it would take to get well: including admit my anger.

Holy Anger

I like the way Margery Williams's book *The Velveteen Rabbit* portrays the idea of becoming real. An innocent, nonthreatening rabbit becomes increasingly soft and cuddly as it is loved. In this season, I was more like a hedgehog or porcupine. God's gut rehab project exhumed not only my grief but also the anger that I had denied for more than three decades.

As a young child, I had concluded that anger was always problematic. Rather than admit my anger, I channeled it into athletics. Thanks to Title IX, I went from sport to sport, playing field hockey, softball, and basketball. I ran track and field in the spring and swam competitively during the summer. This worked until my athletic career came to a screeching halt at college graduation. With no other known egress, the anger pooled in the basement of my soul, damaging the foundation in the process.

In my twenties, whenever I walked past a booth at the mall that sold delicate, glass-blown ornaments, I felt the urge to smash every one of them with a baseball bat. This felt peculiar and out of character. When I mentioned it to a friend, she eyed me suspiciously and recommended I spend some time praying about that impulse. So I did.

Not surprisingly, I gradually came to understand that it was tightly tethered to my subterranean anger. This caused me great distress, because as far as I could tell Christian women did not get angry. If they did, they risked being associated with female dogs or at least accused of being unrighteous. In my estimation, anger and sin were synonymous. No one I had seen ever modeled holy anger. Certainly not those male preachers whose neck veins bulged whenever they pontificated on sin. Their anger always seemed somehow self-righteous and manipulative.

Anger terrified me. I feared that if I dared to acknowledge it, I would be swallowed up by it instantly and irretrievably, never to be seen or heard from again. And yet I sensed that if I wanted to move toward wholeness, I needed to integrate this feral emotion, rather than compartmentalize and deny it.

On a Holy Spirit–inspired whim, I bought two dozen cheap drinking glasses, grabbed a pair of safety goggles, and made my way to an already glass-strewn spot in our urban neighborhood. One by one, I hurled those glasses against the rocks. It was liberating, therapeutic, and healing. Anger still intimidates me, but at least now I can walk past mall tchotchkes without wanting to destroy them.

A Holy No

This gave a needed boost to my healing journey. It also confirmed my suspicion that if I wanted to be whole and holy, I could no longer pretend those unbecoming, broken parts of myself were inconsequential. I had to start confessing my sins.

Unless you're Catholic, confession—as in out loud to another human being—is wildly countercultural. It's humiliating, which, if I'm not mistaken, is part of the point. The potential for future mortification should cause us to pause and ask, *Is this moment going to be worth the shame of admitting it?*

Not only does confession work for me as a deterrent, it helps me recalibrate my internal GPS to Jesus, rather than to my own self-interests—or the misguided opinions of others. To become truly healthy, I have to confess, not only the sins visible to others, but also those that are easily hidden, such as my controlling tendencies and my habit of lying when I am afraid.

I'm still not sure which is more difficult: allowing others to see my failures or the fallout from being honest. Once I started confessing, I quickly discovered that faking health and wholeness was not only easier for me, but often preferred by those around me. My coworkers, friends, and family had all grown accustomed to and comfortable with my facade of niceness.

Facades work. That's why we build them. I was a fearful, insecure child who somehow determined that if I could be perfect and never disappoint anyone, people would appreciate and love me. Perfectionism is not only impossible, it's a brutal, unrelenting master. It drove me to conceal my weaknesses, overpromise, and then push myself to exhaustion in the hope of currying favor with others, particularly those in power. This broken system worked until I was forty. And then I found myself in the midst of a health crisis.

It took two years of appointments with health-care providers and specialists before I received the triple-whammy diagnosis: chronic fatigue, fibromyalgia, and celiac disease. There was no more hiding my limitations, pretending to be perfect, or denying my anger. Nearly every waking moment reminded me of my frailties and forced me to reframe my modus operandi. Ironically, even as my body was falling apart, God was once again stirring the waters, inviting me to experience a deeper healing.

So, when the twentysomething children's pastor informed me that I needed to pull a monthly rotation in kid's church when I was homeschooling my three sons, working part-time, and already volunteering at the church twelve hours a week, I saw it as an opportunity to dismantle the facade of perfectionism. I said I was unable to sign up, she encouraged me to think about my priorities, and then we had an actual argument. Nevertheless, I took her advice. After considering my priorities, I came back a week later to firmly clarify that I would not be volunteering in kid's church for the foreseeable future. I'm sure I lost her respect, but I learned that saying no and refusing to bow down to what someone else wants of me creates space to do what God is asking of me—which, in that particular season, was to get well.

I have noticed that in the church the line between self-care and selflessly serving others is crossed often, especially for women. We intuitively see and viscerally feel when others are hurt or in need. Our natural inclination is to give, and give, and give, until we have nothing left to give but crumbs of bitterness. That experience taught me the power of a holy no.

Finding God—Finding Myself

The author of Hebrews wrote, "God's will was for us to be made holy by the sacrifice of the body of Jesus Christ, once for all time" (Heb. 10:10 NLT). To my limited understanding, being holy does not mean that we hover angelically above humanity, never tempted, never sullied by blood and dirt. If Jesus is "our anthropological North Star,"[5] then to become holy means that we—like Christ—enter not across the stage but through the stable, rife with muck and mess and chaos.

Far too often, self-proclaimed followers of Christ assume that "salvation is a singular, defining event. . . . As much as we might want it to be true, saying yes to Christ does not instantly eradicate all of our sin patterns and make us holy overnight. We become Christians in a process that begins the first time we turn our faces toward him and ends the day he calls us home."[6]

If I understand correctly, in between the first and the final call, I am to willingly, fearlessly choose to become more like the One who was tempted but knew no sin. I am to learn the difference between a self-protective no and a holy no. I am to allow my heart to be broken by the homeless man in the intersection, the displaced refugee, and the orphan tied to its crib. I am to listen until I understand my enemy's suffering—and then actually love that enemy.

Wholeness is so much more than self-fulfillment or self-actualization. Because I have been bought with a great price, I am not my own. I belong to him. In *The Gift of Being Yourself*, David Benner writes, "We do not find our true self by seeking it. Rather, we find it by seeking God."[7] Now, twenty-some years after that embarrassing day at Fenway, I eagerly watch for the waters to be stirred because that indicates God's nearness. When the turbulence comes, I know I will find him. And in finding him, I will find myself.

■ PRAYER

Heavenly Father, please give me eyes to see when you are stirring the waters, and give me the strength that I need to pick up my mat and follow you. Give me an insatiable hunger to risk everything so that I might be more like you. In Jesus's name. Amen.

■ WRITING PROMPT

Describe a time when the waters were stirred in your life. Did you jump in the pool or run away?

This Tree
by Sarah Finch

A strong woman is like
a tree
planted in the desert,
her bark stripped raw from the wind and sand.
In the dry season she waits for
the rain;
her roots
cling to what little solid ground lies underneath the shifting surface.
Her eyes sting with abuse from coarse dirt;
tears fall like dew drops but
her roots
do not give way, even when attacked by
the wind.
Her hope
lies with the scent of
the rain
that always arrives with the storm
which she anticipates with fear and delight.
Her roots
will be tested and the reward will be a quenching of her soul.
The drought ends and she drinks deeply of
the rain.
Her faith
transcends her moment of glory, for when she is finally cut down,
she leaves a legacy—
a seed.

Her mighty shadow is a new shoot,
taking root in soil that knows how to grow a tree
like her.
Rooted in
truth,
she leaves
her traces of
faith
behind.
This tree
will dance
forevermore.

*For there is hope for a tree, if it be cut down, that it will sprout
again, and that its shoots will not cease. Though its roots grow
old in the earth, and its stump die in the soil, yet at the scent of
water it will bud and put out branches like a young plant.*
—Job 14:7–9 (ESV)

■ PRAYER

Lord, help me leave a legacy of grace. Help me weather the storms
that you have sent so that my words and actions will withstand the
temptations and trials of this earth, so that I will not lose hope in your
faithfulness. I pray that the work of faith you have begun in me will
take root and spread. Amen.

■ WRITING PROMPT

Describe the seeds you will leave behind.

Firmly Rooted
by Peggy Mindrebo

After college, I was ready to live a grand adventure with God. *Let's go somewhere exotic; let's do something crazy!* This ordinary life and its goodness was not what I envisioned. I was fortunate to have a good community of women with whom I was raising my children. Our husbands all were busy, and we were good at filling in the gaps with what was lacking in each other's lives. Most of our husbands were medical students and residents in the days before work hours were restricted to eighty per week. My goal when my husband came home was to provide a relaxing place for him. Four children and two adults living in nine hundred square feet made that a challenging proposition!

This was not the life I had thought I would be living. My years at Wheaton College had opened a whole world of ministry to me. I traveled through Europe and remained in Amsterdam as a cook in a Christian youth hostel. There is still a thrill in crafting that sentence; it sounds matter-of-fact, and yet adventurous and daring. I returned and worked for a college ministry in the city of Indiana, Pennsylvania, living with and directing a house of thirty-four college students. Even that sounds a bit edgy, perhaps communal, maybe even bold.

And then I fell in love. Norm was an aspiring doctor who was also doing a master's degree. The new vision for our shared life included two years for the degree, then four years of medical school, five years of a residency, and three years owed to the Air Force. I was pregnant by our first anniversary and went on to have four children. It surprised me how much I loved being a mom. The energy and creativity of it all never left me bored. There were, however, small cracks in my persona.

Back in "those days" it was common for churches to have missions conferences. As I heard their stories, a deep longing stirred within. What about this very ordinary life I was living—had I missed God's calling for me? I had never been one who pined to be married, but it seemed I was very married! I leaned in, cared for my children, and left this unanswered question in the back recesses of my thoughts. Why wouldn't God call me to the life that I was so willing to live, one of service and ministry? Years passed, and soon enough my van was on the road. Soccer, mock trial, cross-country, swimming, track, play practice, youth group, volunteering, and baseball were just a few of our children's activities that consumed me. My friends were living parallel lives.

The sixteen-acre horse farm we lived on was another project that needed my regular attention. Who knew that our starry-eyed idealism would provide me with twenty-one years of work cultivating our land and raising our animals. By the time our youngest was in high school, I was also managing my husband's surgical practice. I stayed on that path for almost ten years. It consumed much of my time and was good in many ways, but it did not touch the longing in my soul.

In the very middle of this life I was living, I added another love. I cultivated this shy desire in the early morning hours. My morning rendezvous were with the likes of Thomas Oden, C. S. Lewis, N. T. Wright, Christopher Hall, Athanasius, and Evdokimov. We met over coffee, and I was entranced. Each one's ideas came to life as I turned page after page. This was not what my friends were doing.

I started distancing myself from these women with whom I had journeyed. I felt judged by them as I felt called to pursue these longings and studies. I rejected them by slowly walking away. This is the pretty face I will put upon this stage of my life. I think the more truthful statement is that I was afraid to live differently than my friends. They were not rejecting me, and I do not believe they were judging me. I just wasn't brave enough to embrace who I was becoming. This was not the first time I had practiced self-rejecting.

In high school, there was a commons area where we would wait before the morning bell rang. There were prescribed places to stand; each of us who had any sense knew our place—the choir/drama group, or the swimmer's group, or the Christian group. I stood on the verge of the cool group. I was not in, and I was not out. No one told me I did not belong, but few missed me when I was not there: a miserable no-man's land. If you remain on the fringes and don't strive to go deeper, you are never rejected.

My adult self did not have enough confidence in my calling to stand in the center, so I moved to the fringe. It was hard to do something that was seen as different, so I did it in stages. As I started seminary, when queried, I would simply state that "I love to learn." A few were bold enough to ask if I wanted to be a pastor. I chuckled dismissively and said, "No." During this time in my life, I was on a number of boards. This was and is an acceptable place for Christian women, even when other doors of leadership remain closed. I was learning that I had something to say and there were people who wanted to hear. That comfortability became unhinged when I entered my Preaching and Proclamation class. I was the only woman in my seminary cohort. The men made a gracious space for me. (Thank God for the Wesleyans!) They had heard my voice on many occasions, and were shocked at how it morphed with my first sermon. I was also shocked. What happened to any authority I might have had? Where was the woman who had a "word from God"?

She had moved to the fringes. What if they reject my stance as a pastor? What if my understanding of my calling was misread? As I looked for a corner to hide in, these men who knew me called me out of the shadows. "Speak," they said. One named Titus was deeply touched by a female voice proclaiming a message for him. He felt spoken to in deeper and richer ways.

While out with some of my husband's colleagues and their spouses, I mentioned that I was back in school (at age fifty-five).

When asked what degree I was seeking, I stated, "A master of divinity." "You're getting a master's of infinity?" a woman asked. Such an outrageous miss in communication was equally matched by an outrageous correction. "Oh no, I am (just) getting a master of divinity." The degree never sounded more unattainable. I will surely never master divinity!

Since those days, however, I have mastered my own story and calling a bit more. My certification in spiritual formation and my training as a spiritual director have made a path for me in the ministry that I now have. My first posture when doing a sermon remains, often, hesitancy. I overcome this by trusting in God's call and reminding myself of the gracious space he has made for me.

And I have circled back. I found the friends that I had left. They rarely ask about my church work or sermon preparation. They just love me. They love my adult children and my grandchildren. We have much in common. I now believe it is okay that things remain unsaid. They are not unkind. They are not standing in judgment. We are each living the life that we feel called to live. As one who loves collaboration, this was a hard reckoning for me in the past. Now, I am comfortable with the "I am for you, but I am not like you" posture that we have with each other. I am learning that I can live out my calling and stand the ground I have been given, while accepting that we have different lenses through which we view the work of God.

I have returned with less "dog in the fight." If these friends can fan the flame of my calling as a spiritual director and pastor, great. If it turns out that our common beliefs and grounding are in other areas, that makes me more sure of who I am. The "time out" that I took has refashioned me. By stepping away and seeking roots that are deeper than my friends' approval or companionship, I have more to offer. I stepped into the unknown and have been transformed by the journey. Ironically, I now have a more generous space for others, even as I have found my own space to inhabit.

The goal of any good hero's story is to return refashioned because of one's adventures, living then for the benefit of others. In literature, it is the monomyth or hero's journey: a departure for adventure, a decisive crisis, a hard-won victory, and a coming home. T. S. Eliot frames it as the hero (or heroine) who returns to where they started, and "knows the place for the first time."[8] I left home in order to return. I had the privilege of circling back to the unfinished business of my own life—that of knowing who I am, knowing what I am called to do, and trusting that God will bring the right companions across my path. I have returned rooted and remade.

■ PRAYER

Father, Son, and Holy Spirit, I am made for community and uniquely called to reflect your image. My dependence upon you is often overshadowed by my desire for others to accept me. Firmly root me in the work you are doing. May I find my place and thrive in your loving call. Amen.

■ WRITING PROMPT

Describe how your journey has been impacted by insecurities and the role community has played in finding your calling.

My Nuclear Waste
by Janna Northrup

I think this whole life is a gift from God to me. Straight Christmas every day.

Just look around at beautiful sunrises or sunsets, the ocean, the mountains, beautiful people and places all around the globe. I love the swallows that float so close to the ground and swoop and make beautiful poetry with the grass. Oh, and sweet conversations with friends—they're such a gift. Then there's my garden, overgrown as it is, and the laughter of the kids in the backyard. Don't even get me started on food, but especially blueberries and coffee.

The more I open my eyes, the more gifts I see. I see the Holy—God's presence—in everything.

Even the work of life is a gift. Being able to use the mind we have, the thoughts that we can share, the ways we can be of use for others, to others. All gift. This is holy, too. I sit and take it in, the goodness of all, the inhabitation of God in the ordinary; it is beautiful and overwhelming and good.

Yet sometimes *(many, many* times*)* I look within and see that I have a heart tied up in knots over the messes in my life: broken relationships, hurt feelings, betrayals of trust, and the ever-present imagining of the worst.

This is my own personal nuclear waste.

I carry it all inside, making me feel wrong and wonky and upside-down. It also keeps me from seeing God's gifts, plentiful as they are.

If I'm honest, I like to dip my toe in that toxic mess that I store in my soul and say to myself, *It'll be okay if I just stir it a little, make it less nuclear waste-y.* So, I do, and I get deeply burdened and heavy and dark and sad and angry.

It doesn't ever work to stir it around. It stays toxic, because I don't have the right equipment to deal with it.

No one does.

And, here, for me, is the insane crazy part about God. He waits nearby me *(Emmanuel* means God with us, always) and says, "Girl, darling one, I want you to give me a gift."

I think the gift he wants from me is my performance. My doing. The pile of accomplishments I feel I need to have for me to be enough. So, I try to give him that, but it never makes me feel like I'm enough.

God, who is ever so patient, says, "No, I don't want your work, your effort." (Even if it is best work and best effort, he loves it but it is not what he craves from me.)

He says, "Give me your steaming pile of nuclear waste."

What?

He wants it. It doesn't make any sense at all, but he is way smarter than me; he knows that the best gifts, the most beautiful things, only come from him. He just wants me to take my worst parts, my greatest fears and weaknesses, the knots in my heart, and wrap them up in some kind of paper with a bow, and say to him, "Here, God, this is yours. I can't do anything with it now. I'm going to give it to you."

I make a mental show of putting the pile, stinky and gross as it is, into an imaginary box or whatever, and I set it down at his feet. I imagine really going into a big room where I can only see the feet of God, big toes mostly, a lot of light and singing, and I set down the horrible "present" I have that makes me burdened and overwhelmed and sad and miserable.

I set it down and take one to two steps away and—I always do this, every time—I run back and grab it again. I start to worry and stew, and the big, painful emotions come back up. So, I hold it again for a while. God waits.

I see that I am not getting anywhere, and now I am covered in excrement. I go back into the big room and put it there again. Maybe this time, I get four steps away before I run back—an addict who needs a fix. I pull it to me again, and feel its familiar burden, and think, *I've got this.*

But, I don't.

This whole process goes on and on and on. But I still believe that the God who gives me so much beauty and hope, and good things, also really wants all my junk. He wants me to give it to him. He wants this stinky present.

Sooner or later, you start to trust God enough. He won't manage it the way you thought he should, but I've learned I can't worry about what he decides to do with it. I just take the minute I am in, and say, *For this minute, I will not try to fix this problem.*

I keep doing that for all the minutes of the day, and as I've said, ad nauseam, I have to go through all the giving it up and getting it back a million and one times.

And, you know, the sparrows and the sunsets, and all that, are even sweeter because I know that *in spite of* the stuff that I keep carrying around, there is great good beauty and holiness still. So, I keep practicing gratefulness for both the amazing presence of God in this world and the even more stunning hope: God wants our garbage, our burdens, and he promises rest.

■ PRAYER

God, thank you for calling me to a life rooted in you and not in my nuclear waste. Thank you for making it so that, because of Jesus, my toxic burden does not permanently damage the soil of my life. Thank you for the rain of your forgiveness, which strikes a perfect pH balance in my soul. Thank you for allowing nothing, not even my most extreme fears and failings, to keep me from the love of God in Christ Jesus. Amen.

■ WRITING PROMPT

Toxic waste is everywhere. Where do you dump yours? Have others
dumped on you?

Trunk

Just a Little More Beauty, Lord
by Heather Creekmore

Just a little more beauty, Lord. That's what I'm asking from you.
I'm not begging for a model's thighs or to wear a slim size two.

Smooth out these rolls, this dimply skin, lift up some sag, if you will.
Wipe out each stretch mark too please, Lord. I know you have the skill.

Just a little more beauty, Lord. Not a lot. It won't be trouble.
Grant me sculpted arms, firmer abs, and a chin that's less than double.

Trim some pounds, while you're at it. Five-to-twenty? You decide.
I don't crave a perfect figure, just a shape I won't have to hide.

Just a little more beauty, Lord. I'm not asking in excess.
A better body to serve you, that's what I'll have when this you bless.

Could you also boost my cleavage? Then, take some cushion off my
   rear.
Surgeons could fix it all, but I'd rather bend the Great Physician's ear.

I know you told the rich man more money will never satisfy.
But, I'm sure that beauty is different, Lord. Maybe I could just try?

I wait and I pray. Yet that scale doesn't budge.
Same stray hairs and jiggly arms. No less pudge.

God, where are you hiding? Can't you hear all I need?
Does not the King of Kings want his daughter to succeed?

Then, in your goodness, you answer my request.
You tell me seeking beauty denies me from your rest.

Chasing beauty won't fulfill. It's a trap, you explain.
"The search keeps us apart, binds heart and soul to what is vain.

I want you to find satisfaction in me alone.
Then you'll release these temporal afflictions you bemoan.

Firmer calves, fuller lips, a bigger bust or fewer grays,
thrill you only for a season. But my love has no limit of days."

"Dear daughter," he continues, "in my image you were made.
Real joy won't come from looking good, earthly beauty always fades.

I designed you for a reason, with great purpose for your life.
Use your body to serve me, not in a quest for, 'Hottest wife.'"

Meekly, I respond. "You're right. A little more beauty would never do.
I chase an idol that promises life, instead of pursuing you.

Forgive me, Lord. For in my sin, I surely miss the point.
A life spent hunting beauty is not the kind you would anoint.

Remove my passion for smaller jeans, straight hair and slimmer thighs.
Instead help me find life in you alone and see beauty through your
    eyes."

■ PRAYER

Lord, help me to see through the shallow promises of physical beauty.
Open my eyes to witness how your beautiful purpose for my life can
transcend the hollowness of the pursuit of a "better" body. Show me
how to derive satisfaction from you alone. In Jesus's name. Amen.

■ WRITING PROMPT

Write a letter to your daughter or a young woman describing true
beauty.

Encasing My Fear
by JoHannah Reardon

I was a frightened child. I was afraid my room was full of spiders when my mother turned out the light. I was terrified that ghosts roamed the streets and were bound to show up on my doorstep. Creepy music sent chills down my spine, and images of ghouls and skeletons turned my stomach. Of all the terrors, the thing that loomed largest was Stranger Danger.

When I was in grade school, a girl in my small hometown was abducted by an unknown man. This sent our community into turmoil and put my small elementary school on high alert. In an effort to keep me safe, my mother frightened me in any way possible, it seemed. It was confusing—because before this incident, she had made light of my childhood fears and repeatedly told me they were nonsense.

Now, Mother painted gruesome pictures of what would happen to me if I were not continuously on my guard against any man I did not know. My impressionable eight-year-old mind struggled. This scary, evil bad guy who was just out there taking little girls took over my imagination and fueled my irrational, lifelong fear of the "evil man."

This horrifying paranoia followed me as I grew older. I found plenty of reasons to support my sense of evil men lurking everywhere. News stories of kidnappings, rapes, tortures, and girls and children sold into slavery abounded. Novels and movies fed my overactive thought life. I perceived the men around me with fear, convinced they all had wicked motives. Nighttime became a terror. It didn't matter if I locked every door and window. Mere glass and wood would do little to stop the "evil man." Every noise and creak meant *he* had managed to get into my home. I knew something was wrong with my paranoid view of things, but I didn't know how to overcome it.

When I became a Christian, I learned God wanted me to trust him with my life. But even that wasn't enough.

God *could* protect me, but I didn't believe he *would* protect me. After all, Bible stories offered little comfort: Joseph was sold into slavery; Jeremiah was lowered into a pit; the apostles were beaten and thrown into prison; and Jesus was crucified—all at the hands of evil men. I read books about overcoming fear, memorized Bible verses that addressed fear, and prayed God would take away my fear, but victory escaped me.

Church became an important part of my life despite my secret paralyzing fears. During my first season of Lent, I began thinking about the value of giving up something for forty days to ensure my dependency on God. Sincerely seeking God's guidance for this process, I definitely heard, "Give up fear and worry."

During those forty days, God did not hold back. He identified and rooted out the ways I fretted and worried. Setting aside forty days to concentrate on this part of my life revealed a hidden sin: the sin of not trusting God—the sin of believing God wanted me to live in a state of waiting for the other shoe to drop—the sin of not believing God loved me.

In the past, I had struggled to move out of my fear. Emotionally I was deeply programmed for fear to be my knee-jerk reaction. But during this sacred season of Lent, I learned to engage my emotions in my relationship with God. It was hard. It was scary. But I did it. I was honest with myself and God.

God immediately began to challenge my commitment to confront my irrational fears. One afternoon while walking in the park, my eyes caught the image of a van seeming to keep pace with me on the road next to me. This is a safe community park, and other people were around, yet my warped instinct was screaming, *Run!*

I caught myself: *I gave up fear for Lent. I do not need to worry about this.*

I continued walking, and the truck pulled ahead.

On a trip to London, my husband and I made arrangements to meet at an outdoor café, but when I tried to find it, I became lost. I stopped each passerby to ask if they knew of an outdoor café with orange umbrellas; none did. My panic rising, I prayed, *Lord, you know where this café is. I trust you to show me.*

Relaxing, I heard the sounds of praise songs wafting around me. A group of college students singing drew me across the street. As I listened, all residual panic washed away. I lifted my head, enjoying the music, and my eyes caught unmistakable bright, orange umbrellas popping up through the trees. Walking to meet my husband, I basked in the glow that God had taken care of me. He knew those college students would be on the corner just when I needed them.

From London, my husband flew to Africa for a mission trip. Normally, the two weeks would have been excruciating for me, mostly because of nights alone. In the past I stacked cans at the front door and locked all the windows so I wouldn't be surprised if the "evil man" broke in. But when my fears began to build the first night my husband was gone, I trusted a good God was standing watch over me, and slept soundly.

Today my husband travels overseas regularly. God in his kindness knew I would need to trust him with my husband's safety, such as on his trip to Kenya when Somali militants killed 147 students at a university. Instead of living in terror, I place him in God's hands and rest in God's goodness.

Those forty days changed my life. I gained a new understanding of who God is and how he wants to relate to me. I daily soak deep into my bones what it means that God loves me and that he wants to care for me. I focus on his character and goodness. Even if something bad happens to me, I know it has been run through the filter of God's love. He doesn't allow anything that is not ultimately for my good, and that is a game changer.

Again, I had this head knowledge before taking forty days to give up fear, but I had never emotionally wrestled with God and let it get into my heart. As I learn who he truly is, I am able to put my trust him. I gain freedom I've never had from my earliest memories.

As a result of that experience and the newfound joy and freedom, I shared my story in a book called *No More Fear: 40 Days to Conquer Worry*. Each day looks at one of God's attributes and applies what that means to our fear and worry. It forces the reader to engage emotions in order to grapple with misconceptions about God. As we understand who he truly is, we are free not only to worship him but to live in delight at being untethered from our fears.

The week I launched *No More Fear,* two men murdered someone in a nearby town and then fled to my neighborhood. General panic ensued as police with guns drawn searched campers, sheds, and unlocked cars. As others around me holed up in their homes, I felt not a jot of fear of those evil men. I would rather have faced murderers than be locked in my prison of fear once again.

I once saw a tree that grew around a piece of iron. The iron looked indestructible, but the tree trunk was so thoroughly wrapped around it that only a small bit of the iron showed. The tree had completely overcome it.

I can't help but see an analogy in that to my fears. I used to wake overwhelmed by what the day held, knowing fears and anxieties would exhaust me before the daylight hours were through. Now, I direct my first waking thoughts to how much God loves me, and I don't get out of bed until that is firmly entrenched in my heart and mind. I picture the strong arms of God's goodness binding my fears. I begin my day with hope and security, which carries me on eagle's wings, as it says in Isaiah 40:31. I soar above the fray, above the terrors of this world, secure in the arms of One who loves me beyond all reason and has no fear of evil.

■ PRAYER

Jesus, thank you for being loving, good, kind, gracious, wise, and in charge of everything. I want to always see you as you are so I can rest safely in your care and not fear all the uncertainties of this world. Help me, as only you can. Let me walk through life confident that you never will let go of me. And plant within me the knowledge of your love so that it encases my fears deep within your goodness. Amen

■ WRITING PROMPT

Paint a picture with words of what you fear most. Where do you see the strong arms of God?

Grief. Sit with It.
by Whitney R. Simpson

They say loss is common in a first pregnancy. The details escape me—specific words said, who knew about the loss, or how many meals were delivered. Yet the gift of the pillow and mug remain clear in my mind over a decade later. As I was cleaning out a closet recently, my gaze fell upon this gift, and I fondly remembered that dark season of hushed loss. I remembered with compassion the "wounded" me who received this perfect gift and the invitation for growth it offered.

The gift invited me to embrace rest after my first pregnancy—a pregnancy that introduced me not to motherhood, but to loss. It was a meaningful gift from a mom who had also experienced a hushed loss and understood this gray season and my feelings of quiet sadness.

While this form of loss is a common occurrence, I had never lost like this; this was different. But it was early in my pregnancy, and somehow the briefness of gestation seemed to discount my grief in the view of others.

The gift of the pillow and mug reminded me that there were people who cared for me and wanted to draw near to me after our loss—even if I did not allow it in my dark time of quiet sadness. I seemed fine on the outside, and few were allowed near enough to know the emptiness I felt within. The gift reminded me that God is near, yet I did not choose to rest or sit with God in my brokenness. While life continued on script, I busied myself and pushed through in fast-forward.

In a few short months—and still giving little time to sitting with the grief—I turned from quiet to angry. It was at my husband's brave urging that I met with someone, months after my miscarriage.

I will never forget the day we sat together on our couch as anger spewed from my lips at him. I do not remember what my anger was connected to that day, but I do know it was unwarranted.

For you see, I could not identify how grief was binding to me and blinding me. Soon, my counselor, and later a spiritual director, helped me process those feelings and not silence or discount them. I discovered God in them, identified new skills, and began embracing the grieving cycle. It was a season of patience that allowed me to process the grief, and, ever so slowly, the anger began to fade.

This processing of the trauma was necessary before I could fill that mug with tea and receive support from that pillow, or from anyone for that matter. I began to sit with God in my grief and discovered I was not alone.

Color soon filled my gray days with the delight and joys of family, life, and ministry. Yet seasons changed as they do, and grief returned with the loss of first a job and later a parent. These losses opened unexpected spaces for anger to return. I stumbled a bit in the darkness, each experience another opportunity and invitation for sitting with God. I was no longer a stranger to the sneaky ways grief masks itself in my heart or in the hearts of others. I was invited to sit in the changing seasons.

Befriending grief has opened me to growth. It walks with me on a journey of spiritual transformation. It teaches me to value others in their times of loss. It helps me to value my feelings and thoughts. It reminds me that God can handle my anger. It invites me to trust those who love me most, even when it hurts. Grief asks that I slow down and sit awhile.

Years later, the little gold pillow and coffee mug invite me to sit with each loss . . . sit with the sadness . . . sit with the longings of my heart . . . sit. Novelist George Eliot reminds me of how vitally important it is to embrace the grief: "She was no longer wrestling with the grief, but could sit down with it as a lasting companion and make it a sharer in her thoughts."[9]

Are you living in fast-forward after loss (even months or years later)? Have you considered the invitation to slow down and sit with your grief for a season? Allow your whispers to be spoken to and heard by the God who weeps with you as you discover grief as teacher, companion, and friend. May you sit with your grief and be comforted by your God there.

■ PRAYER

O God who cries with me, allow me to sit with you. Meet me in those places of sadness that no words or gifts could ever touch. May embracing my own grief reveal the gifts of its companionship as I discover my identity in you, even through quiet or unexpected loss. Allow me in this season to be transformed with hope, delight, and a peace that comes because of your promises and your desire to know me and all of my hurts. Amen.

■ WRITING PROMPT

Journal an experience of loss and where God met you.

When I Wanted Someone to Complete Me
by Amy Davis Abdallah

When I was thirty-two, there was only one thing missing from my life, but that one thing seemed so important that the lack of it darkened all the other good.

I was in a great career—I was teaching theology and Bible to college students and taking them on international trips during breaks. I loved my job. I loved it so much that I had just started a grueling PhD program that would allow me to stay in the career long-term. And what provision I had! The entire program was covered by scholarships and grants.

I was in the best shape of my life—I was a regular at the kickboxing studio and had earned belts in karate. Kicking and punching to pounding music after work felt like dancing to me, making me feel alive. My toned body had boundless energy.

I was connected with friends and family—I had good friends at church, work, the gym, and even the local coffee shop. Though I was sometimes lonely, even longtime friends were just a phone call away, and I made good use of that phone.

But, even with all that, I felt deep, deep lack because I was missing a husband; I was single. All this good was occurring in my life, but I mourned that I was missing someone with whom to share it.

Now, it's one thing to desire marriage; it's another to worship at the altar of marriage, thinking of oneself as lesser without a ring, and feeling as if one's identity is incomplete without a partner. Since no man had told me I was worth committing the rest of his life to, I felt less valuable as a person. I wanted marriage more than anything. I worshiped at the altar of marriage.

So, when he asked me out, I said yes. I doubted it would go anywhere since we were vastly different, but I said yes. And he did all the right things. He romanced me with fancy dinners, flowers, and kind words. The first few months were filled with euphoric beginning-of-relationship feelings, and, being in our thirties, we also spoke of a future together.

Sure, there were his health issues, our communication problems, and significant differences in background, life goals, hobbies, and personal pursuits, but I was thirty-two and wanted a family. He was a good man and wanted it, too. Having dated no one for years before him, I truly thought he was my last chance.

Though the road wasn't always smooth, he got my parents' blessing on our union and asked to put a diamond ring on my left hand. Just days before, we'd had a hard conversation about deep and important relationship things that needed to change, but I still said yes. And so, I found myself, thirty-three, moving toward the long-desired marriage but with a less-than-desirable fiancé.

The inner turmoil this caused made me a rather stressed-out insomniac. On the one hand, I was no longer alone, but on the other, I knew deep within me that we wouldn't make it. Still, I didn't want to let go of the possibility of marriage and children—wasn't this my last chance?

Even more than that, I had given my word. I had said yes, that I'd marry him. Everyone knew of our engagement—though they hid concern behind their words of congratulations. If I couldn't make a relationship work, then I was more of a failure than I'd ever thought. Everyone would know that I was a failure who couldn't keep her word.

When his health took a turn for the worse, I believed I'd be more than a failure—I'd be abandoning him when he was down. How could I walk away? I'd be heartless. And at the end of the day, I loved him.

But I knew that I would not be able to complete the road I was traveling. I tried to end it. I tried to end it right after I said yes. Then I tried to end it a few months later when we were face-to-face. I finally was able to end it over the phone—not only was I a failure, but I was weak.

The grief was deep for so many reasons. I grieved because I loved him and not being with him hurt. I learned that people break up because they can't go the next step with a person, not because they no longer love them. The love remains.

I grieved because I was alone, again. And because I had been filling that loneliness with a person, now it felt worse than ever before. I felt bereft, as if someone had been stolen from me, even though I was the one who walked away.

And I grieved because I was thirty-three and unsure if I'd ever marry. I knew I couldn't be married to him, but there was no one else who'd counted me worthy to say they wanted to spend the rest of their life with me.

As I walked through my deep grief, paying attention to the hurt and processing the pain, the original date of our wedding drew closer, and I decided to have what I affectionately called a "ritual burning." That may sound like a strange practice, but I wanted to get together with friends, process my loss, and make a clean break by doing something physical—burning some objects that symbolized my broken relationship. I hoped the ritual would help me let go of the past and move forward.

I put off mentally processing everything until the last minute. The night before, I wrote a grief journal that revealed what I had lost in the relationship. It was raw and hard to write. I was very nervous when I arrived at my friend's place, journal in one hand and a box of burnables in the other.

My friends and I sat in a circle, I read my journal and explained objects before dropping them in the fire, they encouraged me and prayed for me, and then we snacked on wine and cheese. When we moved to the wine and cheese, it felt so simple and normal—like I was fully accepted regardless, and it was over.

I'll never forget one friend's words that night. She said that, through the breakup, I had finally found my voice. I didn't know my own voice before dating him, but the strength and reality of my voice came alive when I walked away. She was right.

Counterintuitively, in giving up what I thought would "complete" me, I became more complete in myself. I was able to speak what I needed to speak and do what I needed to do at the hardest time. I had given up a coveted dream for a greater reality that allowed me to be fully myself. Even though I still desired marriage, I no longer worshiped it. Even alone, I knew I was valued, and more than that, I valued myself.

And though I thought it would be the biggest failure of my life— this failure to make a relationship work—I learned that failing wasn't as big a deal as I thought. No one around me looked at me as a failure, so why did I think of myself as one? In choosing to "fail" at what I thought was most important in life, my fear of failure subsided, because failure hadn't destroyed me. In fact, it had made me stronger.

My story reminds me of someone in Scripture that we often see as a failure: Martha, Mary's sister. We're so often told to sit at Jesus's feet like Mary—not to be like Martha, who was distracted, worried, and upset about work. Like Martha, I was distracted from worshiping Jesus by my inordinate desire to find Mr. Right.

But though she was distracted, Martha was also great in her own right. Her singleness didn't stop her—she owned her own home, which she opened to Jesus (Lk. 11:38); she hosted numbers of people in her home (Jesus always came with at least twelve of his best friends); and she was a close friend of Jesus (John 11:5).

Like her, after this experience, my singleness no longer stopped or limited me.

And though Martha's not sitting at Jesus's feet is seen as a failure, she's bold in this mistake, and that is good. It's interesting that rather than rebuking Mary directly for not helping, Martha confronts Jesus, telling him to have Mary help her. She could have kept her peace; she could have fumed over the fire and put on a fake smile as they ate, but she boldly rebuked Jesus for letting Mary sit at his feet. While my failure may not have been so bold, it felt bold to me, and it is bold failures that are the easiest to correct.

And I think Martha listened and learned from Jesus, because in the next story where we find her (John 11), it's clear she's a go-getter with growing faith. Her brother Lazarus has died, and she leaves the mourners at her home to meet Jesus on the road. She's learned the "one thing necessary," and goes to learn solely from Jesus. She speaks words of deep faith that are greater than Mary's words in the same situation, and Jesus shares with her and her alone a great "I am" statement: "I am the resurrection and the life" (John 11:25 NIV). Martha declares her growing faith to her friend Jesus.

Though some see Martha only through her failure, a broader understanding of her story reveals her success and how her failure formed her when she listened to Jesus. I love Martha's example; I can identify with her and move forward in hope, regardless of my circumstances.

I had looked down the long-coveted road of marriage, albeit to the wrong person, and learned that it wouldn't complete me, that failure was okay, and that I would be okay regardless. Though I'm sad for the pain I caused, it was only through that pain that I found my voice, that I found myself, and realized she was enough.

■ PRAYER

Jesus, you are the resurrection and the life. In your goodness give life to me, and through my failures make me stronger in order to love you and others better. Amen.

■ WRITING PROMPT

Write about a painful relationship.

Trust God with Our Anger
by Lindsey W. Andrews

On the coldest day in February, several years ago, my baby brother ended his own life. He was barely twenty-nine years old. Because ours was the last conversation he had with another human, the guilt I feel is as strong today as it was in 2014.

I was never angry at him for what he chose that afternoon. The deepest parts of my soul understand his longing for something better. He was a believer in Jesus, but several people questioned his faith after his death. I suppose you can never judge someone for jumping from a burning building until you have been touched by the flames.

There was plenty of anger. I pointed it heavenward. Wasn't he supposed to be holding the universe in his all-powerful hands? With the immaturity of a toddler, I railed in my heart. I stopped short of saying any of those thoughts out loud.

Being angry with God was never allowed in my youth. The small country church we attended in an Oklahoma suburb taught rules. Hellfire rained if disobedience occurred. Conforming to certain conservative political views was required, followed by breathing.

Small-town Christianity gave me a reduced version of faith. As a teenager, I could tell you I believed in Jesus because he was talked about in my daily life. There was a cross around my neck, and larger ones hung in our home. We prayed and asked for blessings over ourselves at meals and offered immediate "bless-yous" for hay fever. I was solid in my faith.

College and on to law school is every conservative parent's dream. God would bless me. Because I believed in every inch of his prosperity, surely it was gospel that security would follow all the days of my life.

Emergencies? I had no plan B if the talisman around my neck should fail. The book of Job was known to me, but never explored. God would surely never stop blessing me, would he? Of course not. I had faith.

Faith is beautiful to talk about until it is the only thing left. How heavy a cross feels when you are carrying it yourself.

I was in my first semester of law school when my brother was in a debilitating car accident. I studied for finals in his intensive care unit, while he was in a coma for seventeen days. Praying he would learn to walk, talk, and function again, my family needed a miracle.

In May of the following year, he walked across the stage, said, "Thank you," and received his high-school diploma. A year later he watched me receive my law-degree diploma. We had made it. We could return to the path of riches and glory, or at least to the sideline of normalcy and routine.

Lifting me up in a giant hug, he twirled me around and told me how proud he was. We glowed. He was an absolute, walking miracle. God had healed him, but no one can look at you and know depression hides deep.

It would take years for him to be diagnosed with bipolar depression. Although my brother was intimate with despair, he hid his symptoms from those he loved the most. He never wanted to feel he had burdened someone with what he carried.

Therapy, inpatient care, meditation, prayer, counseling, and then of course came the medications. While his doctors wanted to spice up his "treatment" with more prescriptions, he only wanted to be free of the cloud he was living below. He was tired of the attention, pain, and disappointment he felt. Relief is an emotion no one understands until you are desperate for it.

When he believed he was out of solutions, he made his last choice. His final text message simply read, "I love you Sister. All of the answers are on my kitchen table." His suicide note solved none of our questions. It only left more to be asked.

A funeral in the Southwest usually includes viewing the body. I put off going to see my brother until the day before the service. I didn't believe seeing a shell of him was going to fix my heart, but my parents begged me to go. They wanted their three kids together one last time. I relented and went.

He was stunning. My baby brother was almost smiling. He looked rested, as if the weight of all his sins was released. I suppose that's because it had been.

I read him verses from Psalms, like I use to do when he was younger and afraid of storms. He no longer needed green pastures and still waters. I would have killed for them. That day in his viewing room, I wept until Dad came in and sat beside me.

"Did we fail him, Sister? Is this our fault?" Guilt and shame rested under my father's eyes. I wondered what his heart must look like.

"No, Dad. Look at him. He is perfect. He would not want us to feel guilty, but all I feel is guilt. Guilt and anger," I sobbed.

"I'm angry too, babe," Dad whispered.

I was hurting. Dad was dying. No one should bury their child, but also, they should never be the one to find the lifeless body. How Dad was still breathing was a testament to grace and adrenaline.

"I'm angry at everything, Dad, everything and everyone. I'm furious with God," I fumed.

"I know. Me too."

We held hands and cried. I have never seen any man cry so bitterly. Surely, I had met Job.

Tragedy elicits two reactions: resolve or complete destruction. Movies and classic literature lead us to believe the best stories are ones where people come together and overcome their situations. The queen is saved, the status quo is restored, and the reel ends with sunsets and victory marches.

For my family, the days and months following my brother's death were more like the Salem witch trials. Everyone who did not point fingers and blame someone else ran into the woods, never to be seen or heard from again. Anger fed into accusations, and frustration morphed into rage. It was easier to blame one another than it was to approach our anguish united. We refused to come together and pushed our anger toward one another.

We have never had another holiday event as a group—because we never heard, accepted, and forgave hard things. We squandered those chances and wondered later why they had passed us by.

Less than four months later, my father suffered a massive heart attack and died after falling into his swimming pool. He was home alone at the time. It was another Sunday afternoon of loss. Another man in my life was gone, and I was livid.

I wasn't sad; I was furious. For the first time I could remember, all I felt toward heaven were fire-filled thoughts of rage. The God of my Sunday school classes surely could not be holding me or my family through this time. He had disappeared and left us in the wilderness.

Since I had preached my brother's funeral, it seemed only fitting to preach again for Dad. My brother's service was Bible verses and visions of hope. Dad's was a celebration of life. I had no desire to put the Almighty front and center. Since he was absent for the tragedy, I felt no reason to give him special recognition. I surely saw no hope on which to speak.

I don't remember sleeping, eating, or exhaling in the days after Dad died. The week before the funeral can only be remembered with tears. Any attempt to pray was thwarted by the steel wall I had placed around my heart.

Standing graveside, I begged Dad to show up. I didn't need God, just Dad. While funeral protocol demands that you stand and smile and console those who show up, I wanted to disappear. I had no words for them, because I had no words for myself.

After several hundred hugs, smiles, and nods, agony fed into the sweltering heat. My husband held my wrist, as I arched an eyebrow.

"I'm checking your pulse. You're going to pass out if you don't sit down soon. Your heartbeat is out of control."

"How fitting," I hissed at him under my breath. "I can't do this. Make these people go home. I want to care and be gracious, but I have nothing left."

Kissing my forehead, he left to find the funeral director. His absence allowed others to crowd into the space. Breathing was unbearable. Smiling was torture.

Please was the only word I could utter in my heart. Whether it was Dad or the Almighty himself, I felt it before I heard it. Peace eased into my soul, like a plant sucking drops of rain. I felt my body relax. There, in the middle of a scorching Oklahoma June day, rain began to fall. Soft at first, then steady, it fell. Everyone dove for their vehicles.

Watching the casket being lowered into the ground, I needed to know this was happening. As red clay hit the top of Dad's casket, I felt more alone than ever before in my life. A piece of soul had left my body. I was a shell where a whole person had once been.

Counseling, meeting with my pastor, and talking through my emotions over the coming months was lip service. I couldn't say out loud I was angry with God. I wondered if I ever would be able to admit I felt abandoned, betrayed. This was not the life I had been promised.

Working out, binge eating, shopping, drinking, crying, being at the office, and writing were my favorite ways to display to the world that I was okay. Productivity was my cover for not having to show real feelings. On days when grief engulfed me, I ran an extra mile, ate an extra donut, and practiced smiling in the mirror. Everyone, even God, needed to know I was fine.

I was failing at everything.

When nothing else works in my life, I pack a bag and experience a new place. For our eleventh anniversary, my husband booked a trip to Alaska. Ten days without kids, responsibilities, and work. It was supposed to be a vacation. It became my wilderness where I wrestled with God.

Whether it is the mountains, the sheer size of the great outdoors, or its wildness, Alaska brings it all to the table. With whales cresting, eagles soaring, and waterfalls at every turn, I lost my vocabulary in Alaska.

Instead of being able to describe what we were seeing, my husband and I would just look at each other and say, "Ooh!" and "Wow!" On the last night of the trip, I sat outside and watched a glorious world sail by. It was then that a rush of anger from the last two years came back. How could the Creator of this place care nothing for my life? Where was the beauty and blessing I was promised as a child?

Then I heard him. The way I did when I was a child in Sunday school all those years before. The voice that made me stand up and say, "I believe." There on that boat, God whispered.

"I know you are mad at me. *Tell* me about it. I made this place, and I made you. I can handle it."

I took him up on his offer.

"If you made all this, why did you leave me? How can you be so precise with creation and so reckless with my heart?" I fumed.

For almost an hour, I railed, and he stayed steady. In his omniscient, patient, firm way, he listened and responded. He brought me to Alaska to meet him again, to question and to be angry. He did it so I would fall in love with him again. Not in the ways of a faith, but in the waves of a relationship.

We try to confine our emotions, perhaps because we are terrified of what may happen if we are honest. *Will we still believe what we have been told all our lives if allowed to question what we know? Is questioning God blasphemy?*

It has taken me almost forty years to realize I can be angry with God. He welcomes my frustrations, as long as I am willing to turn to him. I had to come to terms with myself in anger in order to see God's hand in my circumstances. Inviting him into my anger was the introduction to a new kind of believing.

I grieve my brother and father every day of my life. I suppose I will until my feet enter heaven and I hold them both again. That grief brings me back to 1 Thessalonians 4:13 (NIV): "We do not want you to be uninformed about those who sleep in death, so that you do not grieve like the rest of mankind, who have no hope." I never want to believe I am without hope again.

■ PRAYER

Father, you are good. You walk beside me when I run away and carry me when I deny your existence. Subside my fear with your truth, and override doubt with your cleansing love. I release all of my anger into your hands. All of my tears are counted, cherished, and held. For all of the things that you are, I thank you. Amen.

■ WRITING PROMPT

Have you been angry with God? Write an honest confession and conversation with him.

The Best We Can
by Taryn Hutchison

I set the take-out lunch on my parents' wobbly table, pushing aside pill bottles, lists scribbled on envelopes, and extra pairs of glasses.

"Your daughter's here!" Mom yells down the hallway. Dad's hearing aids are on the fritz, as usual.

"He probably can't hear you," I say for the umpteenth time. "I'll get him."

We meet in the hallway as he wheels himself to the table.

"It's about time! I'm half-starved," my father bellows.

The clock reads 10:30. My parents rise by 4:00 and eat breakfast as soon as they can after taking the first of many pills.

My mother stands, immobile, fridge door open.

"Mom, sit. I'll get the drinks." I busy myself in the one-person kitchen.

"Thanks, honey."

I set down Dad's plate. He immediately takes a bite.

Mom looks at him. "Where are your manners?"

"Huh?"

"You need to wait."

"It's just Taryn."

"Well, that's—"

"Mom, it's fine." I play referee.

I serve up the rest and face my father, speaking loudly and clearly. "You feeling okay about tomorrow?" He will have a carcinoma, and the top of his ear, removed.

"Guess so."

"Well, I'm not," Mom pipes up. "Medicare won't cover it all, and I don't know where we'll get the money. And the next procedure—"

"Mom, don't worry. We can help you."

"Huh?"

"Honestly! Mom. Be patient."

"Patient? That's all I am. Tired of it. I'm old, too." Mom tears up and turns her head away.

I catch Dad's eye. "You'll be like our cat. Tomcats bite notches out of each other's ears. It's their badge of honor."

"Oh boy."

"After tomorrow, the next time will be a snap. You'll be an old pro."

"Next what?" Dad asks.

"I told you. Don't you listen? Don't pretend you forgot!" Mom's voice becomes shrill.

My father cups his hands, shaking from Parkinson's, around his eyes. He hunches forward from osteoporosis. The right side of his body doesn't work well after two strokes. My once-strong father looks frail.

I turn to Mom. "Maybe you told him when he couldn't hear you."

Then I pivot toward my father. "Dad, in two weeks, they'll take another tiny carcinoma off your shoulder. That one'll be easy."

"Why can't they do both tomorrow?"

"I don't know. Good question."

"Because they want to drive me crazy. They want us to go to the poor house. I never wanted to be a nurse, and that's what I've become." Mom's voice rises another octave.

"Mom, do you really think your children will let you starve?" I sigh and collect my thoughts. "Hasn't God always taken care of you? Why would he stop now?"

"You think I worry." Her chin quivers. "But I'm just being a realist."

I get up to clear the table. To my mother I say, "It'll all work out."
To my father, "I'll pray for you tomorrow."
I climb into my car and give way to my tears.

I used to have a large life. I lived abroad and accumulated passport stamps the way others collect shells. After a decade, I returned, partly because of my parents' declining health. I grieved, and still grieve, the loss of my world overseas.

As one of their two children, I volunteered for this. Caregiving usually falls on daughters, and I hadn't paid my dues yet; I never raised a child. I also felt the tiniest bit of guilt because I spent my parents' last good-health decade overseas. My expat missionary adventures cost them—worrying about me in unstable countries during volatile times, missing me—while I blissfully ignored my biological clock winding down.

And so I came home. After my father's quadruple bypass surgery and mother's cardiomyopathy, it wasn't enough to live in the same country; I needed to be closer. My husband and I relocated again, to a town affordable enough for my still-independent parents, and a house large enough to include them, if needed.

Shortly after moving, my father had a major stroke. Mom takes care of him, and we are only a three-minute drive away. My brother helps with financial advice and often shows up with the latest electronic gadget, hoping it'll simplify their lives. It doesn't. New technology just frustrates them. They don't want to see their grandchildren on FaceTime; they want to see them face-to-face.

My world has shrunk. I can't go far, at least not for long.

I first noticed something wrong with my grandmother as a middle schooler. My family lived in a century-old farmhouse; she, recently widowed, lived next door in the small stucco house my grandfather built.

Grandmom puttered around alone all day, drawn to anything living. She had the greenest thumb around and knew the name of every tree. I can remember watching her sturdy four-foot, ten-inch frame haul a huge trunk of a tree she'd cut down by herself. Our dog and cats flocked to her as though she wore a catnip-scented T-bone around her neck. Every Sunday she'd cook a feast, usually pot roast, making a well in my mashed potatoes to fill with creamed corn, just the way I liked it. Afterward we'd have her cake—the best in the world. She invented a frosting just for me with mashed-up peppermint patties.

When our school bus dropped us off, Grandmom would wander over to help me start dinner. She'd weave wonderful stories, taking strands from her childhood in a large German immigrant family in central Pennsylvania and strands from the present, blending the two into one magnificent mess. I remember peeling potatoes and Grandmom demonstrating how to guide the knife toward myself with my thumb. As I perfected my new skill, which did give me more control, she turned the gas burner on and never lit it. When I found her outside, her eyes looked cloudy and confused.

I'd never heard the term *Alzheimer's* before.

Before the disease asserted complete control, we put my grandmother on a plane to visit her daughter far away. My aunt never sent her back. I didn't get to say good-bye to Grandmom. I never asked her how to grow things or make peppermint-patty icing.

What motivates children to take care of parents in their waning years?

Love? Usually.

Guilt? Sometimes.

Family obligation? Always.

I remember Mom fixing my first sewing project—an apron that had me knotted in frustration—while I slept. She invented Color Bingo. I think of her stories. Her creativity. I could count on her to come to every performance, every school activity. She knew more than anyone, won every trivia game, and could talk on any subject.

Dad worked long hours, never made it to any school activities, but afterward, he beamed when I played the piano or recited my lines, just for him. He had skilled hands. He broke a lot of things, but at least he could fix them. He always had an extra twenty-dollar bill to slip me. His regular greeting, "Your car okay?" really meant "I love you," the best way he knew how to say it.

I never doubted it. From either of my parents.

And now. They don't even know the names of my friends. They don't seem to care. Every conversation features them. Their health. Their doctor appointments. Their financial worries. This isn't who they once were.

Sometimes my husband brings pizza to watch sports with Dad, while I take Mom away for a much-needed break. After these outings, she feels refreshed, but I feel more burdened.

My parents have divvied out their treasures to children, grand-children, nephews, and nieces—whenever they see them, never often enough. Mom has filled volumes of scrapbooks with old photographs and memories. She wants her life and her heritage to live on.

My father watches his body fall apart, powerless to halt it. His eyesight. His hearing. He grows feebler every week. He told me he has something for me and my brother in his Bible, just in case. "If you can ever find it," he said.

Mom's issues are more emotional. Her agility makes her appear younger than her age. Medication controls her heart condition. As a Depression baby, she's always worried about money, but lately it's gotten to the point that it seems irrational.

If my husband and I go away, we line up local people in case of an emergency. I can get away from town, but I can't get away from the suffocating shadow of responsibility. When I start to enjoy myself and stop thinking about them, I feel a stab of guilt because of my selfishness.

I try to be selfless and end up dwelling on myself.

What will happen to me when I'm their age? The threat of Alzheimer's haunts me. Sometimes I wonder if I got my master's degree in writing in my fifties to stave it off or prove I don't have it.

I have no children to be the focus of my care. My stepchildren, young adults when I entered the family, have two parents, and I'm not one of them. I found true love too late in life for children.

Then there's my stuff. My artwork. Books marked with notes. Treasures gleaned from countries that no longer exist, a bygone world that still courses like blood through my veins.

Will anyone want these things? Will they want them *because* they're mine? Or will my belongings become a thankless burden, doled out to those who'll never know their stories, never feel their love?

I watch over my parents' final years. Someday I'll do the same for my husband. Who—if anyone—will be there for me?

The first time this fear gripped my heart in its clammy hands, I turned to God. I cried, and he listened. Then he gently reminded me of Isaiah 46:4 (NASB):

> Even to your old age I will be the same,
>> And even to your graying years I
> will bear you!

> I have done it, and I will carry you;
>
> And I will bear you and I will deliver you.

Calm replaced worry that day. I don't need to know the details. *How. When. Who.* All that matters is that God's the one. *He* will do it.

I need to heed the advice I dispense like gumballs to my mother. *Do not fear.* But how? That beloved verse in Isaiah 41:10 (NASB) has the antidote: "For I am with you; Do not anxiously look about you, for I am your God."

I'm transported back to the night the Russian Mafia broke into my flat when I lived alone in Hungary. I repeated those same words, heart racing, until I finally drifted to sleep. Fear began to dissipate when I focused on God instead of what had happened.

Hasn't God always taken care of me? Do I think he'll stop?

Now when I feel anxious, I know what to do. I remember who God is. I rehearse the times I've sensed his palpable presence. I thank him for promising to strengthen and help me. I trust.

My calling in this season includes caring for my parents. This *is* my life. It may not be dramatic, but my voice can rise, unmuted. I can still pick up my pen, type on my keyboard, with new words.

My parents' love for us came through in action. They were present. They were involved. They did the best they could.

That's what I want to emulate. I will be present.

With God's help, I'll do the best I can.

■ PRAYER

Heavenly Father, help me remember your tender care in the past, thank you for your presence today, and believe that you will take care of me in the future. Amen.

■ WRITING PROMPT

Describe a time you were called to be a caregiver and how God tended to your soul.

Silent Sentinel
by Emily Gibson

Our woodlot lies quiet this time of year. Numerous wind storms have snapped trees or uprooted them completely, and they rest where they have fallen, a crisscross graveyard of trunks that block paths and thwart us on the trails.

Years of leaves have fallen undisturbed, settling into a cushiony duff that is spongy underfoot, almost mattress-like in its softness, yet rich and life-giving to the next generation of trees. We've intentionally left this woods alone for over a decade.

When we purchased the farm, cows had the run of the woods, resulting in damage to the trees and to the undergrowth. We fenced it off from the fields, not allowing our horses access. It has been a home for raccoon, deer, and coyotes, slowly rediscovering its natural rhythms and seasons. Now it feels like it's time to open the trails again. We've cut through the brush that has grown up and are cutting through the fallen trunks to allow our passage.

We bought this farm from eighty-two-year-old Morton Lawrence, who loved every tree here. After spending seventy-nine years here, he treasured each one for its history, its fruit, its particular place in the ground—and he would only use the wood if God had felled the tree himself. Morton directed us to revere the trees as he had, and so we have. When he first took us on a tour of the farm, it was in actuality a tour of the trees: large walnuts in the front yard; poplars along the perimeter; antique apples, cherries, and pear; a filbert grove; the silver plum thicket; as well as the mighty seventy-plus-year-old Douglas fir, western hemlock, and red cedar trees reestablished after the logging of the early twentieth century. The huge old-growth stumps still bear the eight-inch notches carved out for springboards on which the lumbermen balanced as they cut away with their axes at the massive diameter of the trees.

He led us to a corner of the woods and stood beneath a particular tree, tears streaming down his face.

"This was where my boy, Lawton, hung himself, taking his life at age fourteen. It was 1967," he confessed.

He stood shaking his head, his tears dropping to the ground. It was clear his tears had watered this spot often over the years. He looked at our boys—a two-year-old in a pack on my back, and the other a four-year-old gripping his daddy's hand—and told us he wished he'd known, wished he could have understood his son's despair, wished daily there was a way to turn back the clock and make it all turn out differently. He wanted us to know about this if we were to own this woods, this tree, this ground, with children of our own to raise here.

I was shaken by the sacredness of the tree. Lawton lay buried in a nearby neighborhood cemetery, a too-young almost-man lost forever for reasons he never could express to others. Still, it was as if this spot, now hallowed by his father's tears, was his grave. It was this tree that witnessed his last act and last breath on earth.

We left the woods untouched until now in our effort to let it restore and heal, and to allow that tree to become redeemed by new growth and life.

We tell Lawton's story to our children, reminded of the precious gift of life we have been given, and that it must be treasured and clung to, even in our darkest moments. Morton's tears watering this woods are testimony of his own clinging to precious life, through his faith in God and in respect to the memory of his beloved boy. Morton and his wife, Bessie, now share the ground with Lawton, reunited again a few miles away from our home that was also theirs.

Their woods are reopening to our feet, allowing us passage despite the darkness that overwhelms it each winter. These tall and silent sentinels harbor life amid the dying as a forever reminder that spring comes again.

And we will not forget.

■ PRAYER

Our Father in heaven, remind me in my darkest moments that your gift of life is precious. When I weep in anguish and in times of pain, may I remember the tears shed by your Son. Help me believe my faith will survive the darkness and will rise again through your Spirit. Amen.

■ WRITING PROMPT

Describe a time when you had to fight for your faith.

Emergence
by Sharon R. Hoover

Under beige tented sheets and flashlight's dull glow,
words travel heart to ink to diary's welcome pose.
My spiral companion held childhood's harsh side
friend betrayals, chicken-legs, and depression untold.

Under academics' fluorescent light my words journeyed on
Numerous essays, poems, and short stories I did pen.
My writing shaped, yes
yet in templates and frameworks my true voice lacked home.

Under stars, one Fall eve, Master Creator dropped in
courage awakened my numbed heart, my muted soul.
A new journey seemed possible, word by word I hoped to go,
soon images begged voice and ponderings sought ink to now flow.

Beside the path spread a welcoming Redbud writerly tree,
heart-shaped leaves nurtured roots and community.
Like-minded souls traveled side by side
in valleys less lonely and the road wider still.

Beside travel companions I flourish anew,
insecurities released from hidden places since found.
Writers with voice and passion my new kindred mates
dispensing wisdom and trail mix on the journey we roam.

Above the keyboard my fingers do fly,
staccato keys toil as pensive journeys materialize.
Uncovering the mystery of trail's twists and frequent turns
God's work revealed, the scales since long gone.

Above the noise, my voice starts its rise
Amplified by travel companions emptied of pride
Beyond care of critical eyes I write with freedom and joy
Now journeying, yet sheltered, under the Master's family eye.

■ PRAYER

Lord God, I praise your name and your revelations within me. Where
now can I go to express my heart and art and imagination? Lead me
to a place of grace where I may find encouragers and equippers and
accountability-keepers. Free me to explore this world with flare and risk.
O Lord, my Strength, help me then to pour myself into community
and away from pride, loneliness, and a voice devoid of truth. In Jesus's
name. Amen.

■ WRITING PROMPT

Describe your hope for an authentic, creative community. What does
that look like?

Stories and Scars
by Mallory Redmond

slammed the door of my car and ran up the front steps of the yellow house I had grown up in, tears streaming down my face. Frantic, I hurried in and out of different rooms looking for someone—anyone—to hold me together.

This yellow house is where I lost my first tooth, climbed incessantly up the door frames, and conspired with my sister to try and convince our brother to let us give him makeovers. On this night, it is the yellow house where my mom cradled her twenty-four-year-old daughter like a helpless infant, wailing from the pain of a freshly broken heart.

"I'm broken, Mom," I sobbed as gigantic tears fell from my tired eyes. "I'm all broken."

Forever Marked

Just six months before that gut-wrenching night in the yellow house, I was face down on an emergency-room stretcher, desperate for a different kind of healing. An at-home accident had left me lying in a pile of glass that had once formed a coffee table. My boyfriend reacted quickly, scooping me out of the shards, but not before I was severely injured. While he was in a nearby hospital bed with a wounded hand, a doctor was closing my gaping back with thirteen stitches.

I shared something terrifying, and therefore unifying, with my boyfriend—the man I was certainly going to marry—on that traumatic night. I only felt more connected to him through the panic and survival of the accident. However, while the scar—eerily shaped like my boyfriend's first initial—will last my lifetime, the relationship did not. The breakup that led me to my mother's embrace several months later was just as chaotic and painful as that night we were at the mercy of thousands of pieces of glass.

Now, I am marked. Even if I felt able to pretend this man had no impact on me, the jagged scar on my back exposes the truth: I have been forever changed, visibly marred, painfully undone. I cannot erase the scar on my back or the break in my heart.

Our breakup disoriented me—shattered the plans and expectations I had for my life. I didn't *want* my circumstances or self to be transformed; and yet, without my authorization, everything was changing—from the skin on my back to the comfortable path I had planned for my life. I was silent and stagnant, waiting to hear from the man I had envisioned a lifetime with—waiting for us to work it out like I knew we would.

But the phone never rang. We never spoke again. My worst nightmare was my reality: he was gone and I was in jagged pieces. I didn't know how to "do this"— how to take all of my broken pieces and put them back together in a way that could resemble a whole and healthy person.

It Still Works—It's Just Cracked

The wall of the family room in that yellow house I grew up in has always held a weather center displaying the time, temperature, and barometric pressure using brass-finished instruments encased in glass portholes. It was a piece of art more than a point of reference for detailed weather information, but it was a meaningful piece for my parents—a wedding gift, traveling with them to new homes and bearing witness to their growing family from its place on the wall.

In my adolescence, when I performed endless gymnastics routines for my unenthusiastic audience of siblings, I would often walk on my hands, rather than my feet. I still remember the day when, walking into the living room in a handstand, I lost my balance and my heel hit the glass over the thermometer of the weather center. I cracked the glass but, thankfully, nothing shattered, and I walked away—on my feet—unscathed.

Although my body was unharmed, I braced myself for my mom's reaction to the now-cracked wedding gift. When I finally mustered up the courage to tell her, she was surprisingly unfazed. "It still works," she said, matter-of-factly. "It's just cracked."

What I couldn't comprehend the night my mom consoled me in the room with the cracked-not-broken thermometer is that I might be only cracked, not broken. I couldn't imagine that I could still "work"— would it be possible that the tears would stop? Would I laugh, engage with others, and take risks again? Can someone as cracked and scarred as I am still stand tall, use my voice, and offer something of goodness to the world?

Still Becoming

Last summer, I was sinking deep into awe as I walked through the redwood forest in Northern California. How small we humans are next to the giants of the redwoods.

No two trees are exactly alike. Many are the same species, of course, but they each are changed—by age and experiences—in their own way. They may be damaged by the scars of a disease, marked by the unforgiving pecks of wilderness creatures, or wear the carved initials of two spirited lovers. As I wandered through the great big forest in my tiny body, these trees—scarred, marked, and carved—towered above with great strength.

And there I am, hand in hand with my husband—a man I met six years after the heart-wrenching breakup—my back still carved with the first initial of my first love. Over time, it has happened: I am okay. I have found new life after the death of that relationship; I am not broken, just a little cracked. I certainly am not unscathed, but I can still be seen, heard, and used as a vessel of God's truth and grace.

What has fallen apart can be put back together—certainly not always in the way we desire or imagine, but often in a manner that teaches, strengthens, and refines us. Our scars, the ones on our hearts and our bodies, help make our stories; they are not *the* story—dictating how it will all end—but they add a chapter or several. They are like little circles, spread out along the map of our memory: *You Were Here, You Were Here, You Were Here.*

What this sorrow and healing have shown me is that we do not break—we become. We ache, wail, bruise, bleed, dance, laugh, and stumble into more of the person we were created to be. We will not make it to the end of our days without many stories and some scars— and I think that means we've lived big and brave lives. Through pain, we may grow into people who carry God's grace, empathy, wisdom, and faith because we were emptied of whatever earthly thing or being we had given ourselves over to.

This experience continually brings me back to the Cross—the place where the Son of God endured the utmost pain and suffering. There was grief and wailing, and there were deep scars on the hands of the One sent to save us—but the ultimate redemption story followed that traumatic evening on the cross. A new story unfolded out of the ashes: because of the scars Jesus received in his death, we have been given new life.

It was true back then, and it remains true today: God redeems, even when we feel shattered and unredeemable. He works in the cracks; he mends, stitches, redirects, teaches, and saves us. Where we feel grief and death, he can introduce us to hope and renewed life. It doesn't happen immediately. It might take three days in a tomb or six years in a therapist's office, but not one of us is beyond saving.

It was only when I cracked that I was able to see how God could heal and empower me. To stand in his redemptive strength may mean showing how scarred, marked, and carved we are—but stand tall, anyway. Isn't it an honor to share that quality with the giants of the redwoods?

May you come to bless your scars—after all, they are only a part of your transformative story, and it's not over yet.

▪ PRAYER

Jesus, I am so grateful that you are a God who works in the cracks. Thank you for using me to expand your kingdom, even though I am marked with scars. I ask that you show me how I can bring forth light and life, even if I'm feeling darkened and broken. Help me to believe my scars are only a part of my redemptive story—not the end of it. Amen.

▪ WRITING PROMPT

What are the cracked-not-broken parts of you that still work to reflect God's redemption in your life?

No Story Wasted
by Bronwyn Lea

Deep in the redwood grove is an ancient tree. At nearly three hundred feet, the sequoia had once been a majestic tower. Now, it lies fallen. A photo backdrop.

Families line up, and when it is our turn, I trace my fingers from the center of the tree to its edges. This tree is over two thousand years old, a sapling when Jesus was born.

"See this?" I motion to my daughter, enfolding her fingers in mine. "Each one of these rings represents a year. Some years this tree went through a fire, as you can see from this scar here. See where the rings are close together? Those were drought years when the tree had to shore up all its reserves. Each ring tells a story."

Sapling

*A tree getting lots of sunshine and
rain will show rings that are relatively
broad and evenly spaced.*

Josie was always the girl asked to give her testimony. Abandoned at birth, shuttled between foster families, and then finally adopted—she bore deep scars.

The story of God's grace changing her life in her teens was miraculous, leaving people breathless.

However, it also left many student listeners feeling as if they had no real testimony of their own to share. Compared to Josie's, their stories felt tame and unspectacular.

"Don't underestimate how extraordinary your testimony is. If you believe in Jesus, you have experienced a cosmic rescue worthy of the Avengers."

Often, these were students of remarkable maturity. In situations of conflict, they were less likely to lash out. When battling trials, they were more tethered and anchored than those who had not been as well-nourished in their youth. There is no boring testimony.

The Forest

If growth appears to have slowed, it's possible
that the neighboring trees are providing too much shade,
while their crowns and roots are taking up the
lion's share of water and sunshine.

Yearbooks are fascinating. Each face is unique, but also reveals commonalities. The fifties had bomber jackets and sweetheart necklines; the late sixties had long hair. Hairstyles in the eighties could not have been higher.

A trip to the mall highlighted this decade's winter look for women: boots over leggings or skinny jeans; a longish cardigan; long, curled hair. I saw several dozen teens dressed in this "uniform" and amusedly realized I myself was also wearing boots over skinny jeans and had curled my hair that very morning.

We are, without question, creatures of cultural osmosis: absorbing preferences and prejudices from around us. It often takes both time and distance for us to recognize this influence; gaining perspective can usually only be done in retrospect.

Travel can unseat our expectations of normality: moving away from one's hometown and coming back again, you feel the shift that comes from experiencing a new climate.

Seeking out the stories of those unlike us, and with whom we disagree, is another way to fight the effects of cluster growth.

The Clearing

After removing crowding trees, you'll see wide,
evenly spaced rings which indicate that the tree is
growing rapidly and straight once more.

I went into motherhood expecting a time of spiritual drought. After years of vocational ministry and a rich spiritual diet of study, prayer, and witnessing the Spirit at work, I anticipated that maternity leave would mean switching from go-go-go to idling in neutral.

I did not expect God to show up in the nursery, whispering to me that the tenderness and love I felt toward my baby was just a fraction of how he felt about me. How her dependence on me was just a fraction of my dependence on him.

The Spirit met me in the silent spaces. In the wild and surprisingly solitary clearing of motherhood, God showed me an artesian well I hadn't known was there and whispered, "Plant yourself here, my thirsty one. Blessed is the one who walks with me: she is like a tree planted by streams of water, she yields fruit in season, her leaves do not wither" (see Ps. 1:3).

Fire

A fire in the forest can be easily seen by scarring on the tree's bark.
Year by year, the tree will create more and more
wood to cover the scar, but it remains
in the tree's history.

Kristen explodes into a room. Trendy, vivacious, a wit that would be obnoxious were it not for her deep-seated humility, she is a kaleidoscope character. I love being her friend: she is always ready to encourage, help, cheer . . . all in coordinated outfits.

For those like me who are easily intimidated by extroverted and fashionable people, Kristen may not have seemed a good candidate for my friendship. She had it too together, I thought.

But Kristen and I have this in common: we've seen each other's scars. Of course, we didn't show them when we first met.

Our paths crossed when our children became friends, and it seemed like a good idea to carpool to shared activities. It didn't take long before Kristen dropped the "mom facade." Her baby-in-waiting was a miracle baby, she said. The one God gave her as a sign of hope for her marriage.

After two kids and a dalliance with substance abuse, her husband confessed to an affair. In the midst of her heartbreak, she heard God speaking to her: "You have the freedom to leave, but if you stay, I will redeem this."

Her confidence in her husband shattered, she chose to hear God's words. She told me she railed and wailed through that first year, wondering how to rebuild trust and heal her gaping wound. A few months later, she found herself pregnant: a son of promise, she said.

It's been ten years now, and Kristen has four kids. She's still married. Still the extroverted, vivacious woman whose laugh was captured in her college photos. She's become a refuge for women who are facing betrayal, a cheerleader for those who don't know if they can forgive, a prayer warrior for those who wonder if they'll ever heal.

When my marriage goes through one of its inevitable bumps in the road, I know who to call: the one who has been through fire and lived to tell the tale.

Drought

Narrowed rings that go on for several seasons
can indicate a drought. Few things can slow
a tree's healthy growth like prolonged lack of water.

Cadie was what you might call a girl who was "plugged in" during college. An older friend from high school took her under her wing when she arrived on the college campus and introduced her to maniacally extroverted types. She joined a small group, went on retreats, found a community, and experienced growth and vitality in her faith. At the closing meeting in her senior year, she told her college group the myriad ways she had seen God's faithfulness. She was stretched, fed, and fueled for a life in his service: ready to meet the world.

Cadie luckily secured a paying job shortly after graduation. She bid her roommates farewell and drove two hundred miles south, where her adulthood would officially begin. Cadie called her parents and friends daily, initially. Settling into a new home and job was hard work. On the few weekends that were free, Cadie threw her purple tote into the backseat and headed north to visit friends and family. Within six months, Cadie had found a new rhythm: she had found friends and had turned her casual interest in rock climbing into a serious sport.

It was only when Cadie took her first vacation after a year of work and planned a five-day climbing trip with friends that she noticed. She sighed, and her climbing friends offered a penny for her thoughts. She answered: "I'm remembering a verse from the Bible, about how God made all these stars, and how amazing it is that he still notices us." She looked around at the circle of stunned faces. Mark spoke first: "I didn't know you were into God," he said.

"I am," she answered. "Or at least, I was." She blinked back tears and breathed in sharply.

"I still am," she said. "It's just been a while, and I didn't notice until just now how much I've missed him."

Reaction Wood

*Rings that appear wider on one side than
the other may indicate that something pushed
against the tree as it was growing. The tree
will build "reaction wood" to help
support the side that's leaning.*

When experts said that stories of our families of origin are woven into our present, I thought: *Poppycock.* But fifteen years and ten thousand miles apart from my sisters, I found myself irrationally upset and insecure over the fact that we'd all be under the same roof again in a matter of days.

I began obsessing about little things: my toes were hairy; my eyebrows needed shaping. An hour in front of my wardrobe yielded nothing to wear. We were traveling halfway around the world, and there wasn't even a pair of pajamas I wanted to pack.

My husband was dismayed. I was inconsolable.

My best friend stepped into the fray. "What's going on here?" she gently asked.

My fifteen-year-old self launched a meltdown in my thirty-two-year-old body: I didn't feel pretty next to my sisters, never had. They were well-dressed, well-toned, well-traveled. They wined and dined in Paris, London, and Venice. Stories of art, museums, boys, and that time they baked "herbal" brownies and Mom unknowingly ate one.

I, on the other hand, worked for a church. I had had sex with exactly one person: the man I married. I had chosen my life, my friends, my hobbies; and on any given day, I would have told you I loved my life, filled as it was with grace and laughter.

But on the cusp of a trip back to my childhood home, I was panicked: What if the life I had wasn't the life I had chosen? What if I had this life simply because I wasn't cool enough, or beautiful enough, to have had any other options?

Saying it aloud did bring perspective. Yes, my sisters and I have made different choices. I am now very grateful for mine.

We went through stuff, my sisters and I: family drama, multiple schools, moves—and in each season we played a part in one another's stories. Often, I played the grown-up. Middle sister played the mediator. And the baby of the family countered my idealism and highbrow ethics with profound common sense and wisdom. Perhaps, like a teepee of kindling sticks in a fire, if you lean the three of us together, we fit just right—more stable than any one of us might have been alone.

Every church community I have belonged to has ranked among its top priorities discipleship and mentoring, including helping women connect with each other—younger and older—in faith so that they might grow together.

There is no shortage of young women longing for these types of relationships. They are hungry for the caring, attentive wisdom of the women who have gone before them. Eager, but afraid of the unknowns: How can they initiate these relationships? Will they be accepted?

The trouble proves to be finding women willing to serve as mentors. Those I've spoken to feel inadequate: battling as parents, hitting glass ceilings at work, dissatisfied with retirement, dealing with midlife-crisis pressures.

"What could I possibly have to offer?" they protest. "I don't even feel like I've worked out the answers in my own life, much less feel able to work out somebody else's."

But here is the surprising thing we learn from the tree: We know more than we think. We have lived through more than we acknowledge. We are stronger than we realize. Each of our experiences adds a ring to our tree. Some years have little growth, some abundant, but always: growth.

That relationship you made bad mistakes in? There is someone who may need to hear that their mistakes do not define them. That trauma you lived through? There's someone in pain who needs to talk to someone who knows what it's like.

There is a generation of saplings who need a forest of people with their many-storied rings, each telling of God's redeeming grace.

No story is wasted; no ring is added without building strength.

Lean on me, we say to each other. *See how long we have stood? By God's grace, we will stand a little longer.*

■ PRAYER

Heavenly Father, thank you for all the stages of life depicted in photo albums, scrapbooks, and notes tucked away. You know the pieces I have kept and the ones that mark me. Lord, inspire me to "forget not all [your] benefits" (Ps. 103:2 NIV), keeping a record of your work in my life. Thank you, gracious Father. Amen.

■ WRITING PROMPT

Record God's work in your life based on this statement: She is like a tree planted by streams of water.

Branches

Caretakers of the World
by Shayne Moore

Women and mothers care for their children and their families—we are the caretakers of the world. When someone is dying of AIDS in Africa, it is a woman who is by the bedside; a mother, a sister, an aunt, a grandmother, a daughter.
—Princess Kasune Zulu

The relentless rain pours down. Nothing here is built on level ground. Brown, dirty foam forms where the water is pooling in the waiting area outside the hospital. If the building was once level, perhaps over time this assault of rain has eaten away at the dilapidated structure and surrounding compounds.

Today I am observing a Kenyan nurse named Nettie, fluent in English, Swahili, and Kipsigis. I attentively stay one step behind, hoping to learn, yet self-consciously trying to stay out of her way. Nettie moves slowly around the waiting area with her clipboard, writing down names and speaking to the many people who braved the storm. She helps an elderly woman find a seat, answers endless questions, and laughs with the Kipsigis grandmothers and their grandchildren.

I am not a health-care worker, a missionary, or a government agent. I am fluent in exactly one language. I am a stay-at-home mother with three young children who is in Africa with my church. The African Inland Mission is building a new hospital in rural Kenya, and a team of us from my church are here to do some light carpentry and painting and to learn about the local HIV and AIDS programs.

It has been three years since I first heard of the devastating effects of the HIV and AIDS global pandemic. It has been three years since I first grappled with the statistics: 5,000 children die every day from severe diarrhea; 72 million children (56 percent of whom are girls) remain out of school around the world; every day in Africa 4,400 people die from AIDS; and more than 12 million African children have lost one or both parents to AIDS.

Now the statistics have faces and names.

I silently follow Nettie as I marvel at the earlobes on the Kipsigis grandmothers. Nettie catches me midgawk. She explains that the tradition of stretching out women's earlobes was abandoned several generations ago, but it can still be seen on older women. Some of the women are dressed in traditional tribal attire, and their ears are so stretched that the circle of flesh reaches down to their shoulders. Nettie chats with them, and I greet them the best I can. We grab hands and smile.

The people look to be on the verge of falling apart, with rotting and missing teeth, growths on their faces, discoloration of the whites of their eyes, and tattered scarves wrapped around alarmingly thin bodies. The absence of consistent medical care is evident at a glance.

Most have traveled a long way to this rural hospital. Cars are scarce—some have bicycles for the difficult roads, but most people walk everywhere. They come with a variety of ailments: a four-year-old boy with a donkey bite, a five-year-old with a snake bite, a little girl named Daisy with a horrible case of malaria.

Some have come to the Volunteer Counseling and Testing Center (VCT) to be tested for the HIV virus. These clinics are supported by the Kenyan government to encourage people to find out their HIV status. The hospital is staffed by nine counselors, all women, who serve this community.

Nettie explains, "Knowing your status is the first step in arresting the spread of HIV and AIDS. Most of my patients are men, as women fear finding out their status because they will be turned out and shunned by their husbands and families and separated from their children."

She tells me this without emotion, but my brain and heart are having a hard time processing it. This is not the first time I have heard about the immensely troubling double standard for men and women regarding HIV and AIDS.

I am a woman from America, and my paradigm for the role of women in society is Western, modernized, and egalitarian. I am trying very hard not to be ethnocentric as I reflect on what I am being told about women, HIV, AIDS, and extreme poverty in Africa. I want to respect the culture and traditions of other people, but this doesn't feel right.

If knowing your status is the first step to arresting the spread of HIV, and women aren't tested, how will the disease be stopped? If a man brings HIV into his home because of infidelity (brothels are common in rural Africa, and men often contract HIV from sleeping with prostitutes), then gives it to his wife and children, how is it okay in any culture for that man to throw out his HIV-positive wife?

From Nettie I learned that in this part of rural Kenya, girls are often sexually active at the age of twelve and boys at eighteen. Within the VCT's client base, more men come in for testing, yet more women are HIV positive. Partly this is a result of how a woman is made; she is physiologically more susceptible to contracting the HIV virus.

Nettie also confirms the horrible stories of rape on very young girls, telling me that in western Kasum, an area outside of where we are in Litien, the nurses and home-based caregivers report frequent cases of rape because men believe that sleeping with a virgin will heal them of HIV.

I had traveled the day before with Nettie to Cheborgei, a village forty-five minutes away, where the hospital and community have a home-care group. We are in Kenya during the rainy season, and although the sky is clear, the outrageously bumpy roads seem more like drainage ditches, and we are jostled and jerked in the back of the 1950s enclosed pickup truck as we wind around the tea fields to the old mission church where the villagers gather.

Upon arrival, my body feels bruised, and I untangle myself from the cramped rear of the truck. Nettie and I are greeted by a group of men. The chief of the village is contagiously exuberant. His loud voice booms across the lawn of the church: "God is great! There is no one like our God. We! Are! Happy!"

Tears prick my eyes at the unexpectedly joyful greeting—and this for an AIDS education meeting. The happy handshakes, greetings, and smiles are extended all around.

An old mission church stands at the center of the small village. The homes have dirt floors, and the walls and roofs are made of sticks lashed together with rope. The church is the only modern structure, and it looks frozen in the 1940s. I half expect to see a white missionary come around the corner dressed up like that lady in the movie *Out of Africa*. It appears the missionaries who built the church and educated this small community have since moved on, but they left behind yellowed posters of Jesus and his disciples, a pile of mildewed hymnals, and an old wooden cross.

Yet this place is alive. Newly planted flowers color the path to the front door. The floor is swept, and the smell of fresh chai tea fills the sanctuary. A bright, clean tablecloth is on the altar. The villagers smile and chat together. The women are talking about something with great passion, and I wish I could understand what one woman seems to be explaining to the others.

About fifty men and women have gathered to hear Nettie teach about HIV and AIDS: how it is transmitted, how to avoid infection, how to practice family planning, and how to avoid infecting children. Once inside the church, the men and women separate themselves, with the men seated on the right and the women on the left.

As a former junior high teacher, I observe that Nettie is a skilled teacher. She has an easy, yet authoritative rapport with the villagers. She is stern, direct, gentle, and subtle all at the same time.

Nettie flows effortlessly between three languages, English, Swahili, and Kipsigis, and as she speaks, her eyes glow with tangible warmth and power. She is a mother of four, and her community calls her "the mother of all." She and I are both thirty-five.

Standing at the pulpit, Nettie asks, "We talked of this last time. Can someone tell me how HIV is spread?"

"HIV is spread through sexual intercourse and needles," a man volunteers from the male side of the church.

As Nettie continues her questioning, most people seem to know the textbook answers. I do wonder about the probability of needles being a problem, as it seems just finding a container to carry water is difficult in this far-flung place.

"I have another question for you," Nettie says. "What do you do if your wife is HIV positive and you are not?"

The church is quiet while people shift uncomfortably in their pews. Nettie looks to the women with hopes of engaging a response from the female side of the church.

No one speaks.

Finally, a man says matter-of-factly in broken English, "If your woman, your wife, has got the HIV, you leave that wife behind and marry another."

Nettie is very composed—this answer does not surprise her. But me? It takes everything in me not to fly out of my pew and tackle this man. I want to stand on the altar and scream, "No! No! No!" Instead, I hold back burning tears and try to control my breathing.

At the pulpit, without missing a beat, Nettie directs the same question to the women. "What do you do if your husband is HIV positive and you are not?" Several women indicate a willingness to abstain from sex. I wait, confidently hopeful one of the ladies will push back on what the man said.

Instead, the room is painfully silent. An older woman finally speaks. "If you are married and you cannot . . . " She giggles as she cannot seem to say the word *sex* in mixed company. Several uncomfortable chuckles follow. "I mean, if you don't have that, what do you have? All you have is cooking and eating."

Everyone laughs as the painful truth is solidified through the safety of comic relief and shared experience. I watch Nettie, who persists, "What do you do if both of you are HIV positive? Do you have a baby?"

With the nodding of heads and murmurs, the room unanimously seems to say, "Of course."

Nettie sensitively points out, "I'm not telling you not to have a baby, but the baby will be infected, and now you have more trouble in your house."

This sad exchange is pushing down on my shoulders and my soul. I drop my head to hide my tears and notice a tattered Bible being held tightly by the woman sitting next to me. I glance up at her to see an ancient and lovely face. The wrinkles etched into her ebony skin tell a tale of a long and beautiful life—how old she is. Her beauty catches me midbreath, and I almost make a noise trying to breathe again. How old is her Bible? Was it her mother's? Her grandmother's? The cover is ragged, and the pages are crumpled and yellow.

I am surprised by how much her act—bringing her Bible to this meeting—moves me. She is far past childbearing years. This strange new virus has brought death to her village and new reasons to gather in her place of worship. A lifetime ago, had she watched this church being built, when strangers brought a new message to her people? Did she once walk to church holding her mother's hand while clutching this treasured Bible in the other?

I do not dare lift my head again as I try to hold in my tears. I keep staring at the Bible and at the ancient feminine hands holding it. They are my lifeline to sanity, or at least cultural appropriateness. Her hands—strong, callused, feminine hands—are keeping me from collapsing on the floor or jumping up to organize the women into some kind of rebellion.

At this church, in this village, the statistics have names and faces.

Today at the VCT, we have moved under the lean-to waiting area, and Nettie is shouting to be heard over the rain. I position my feet between two puddles, hoping to stay dry as I listen to the deafening noise of the rain on the tin roof. The woman who Nettie is helping seems to be about my age, and a small boy clings to her side. I look down at him, making eye contact, and smile. He looks at me with huge brown eyes, unsmiling, before looking away and pushing into his mother.

Nettie hands the mother a piece of paper. Taking her son by the hand, she walks over to the cutout hole in the plywood wall, to the hospital pharmacy. I see her get some medication and hurry into the rain. I watch her leave, clutching the medication to her chest.

"Nettie, what did you give her?" I ask. "Medication for HIV?"

"Yes." Nettie nods. "She got her ARVs today. She has enough now for this month."

Antiretrovirals (ARVs) are used to treat retroviruses like HIV. Only 3 percent of Africans have access to these lifesaving medications, and their availability in rural Kenya surprises me.

I am excited and hopeful. "Where did they come from?"

"The medications came from the government. Every VCT is allotted a certain amount of ARVs, depending on their need and if they meet the set criteria," Nettie patiently explains.

"They came from the government? Where did the government get them?" I am still fascinated because I have been told not even governments have good access to these medications.

"The government and the pharmaceutical companies they work with, recently received a large grant from America. PEPFAR money. Do you know what that is?" Nettie asks.

I let out a quick, surprised sigh. I know about PEPFAR because I lobbied for it as Congress and President George W. Bush created the President's Emergency Plan for AIDS Relief. I called Congress and the White House to urge the passage of this bill, which was signed into law.

I freeze as I watch the mother and her son disappear down the road. How can I feel such a sense of solidarity and difference at the same time? We are both mothers, but I have rights and options in my culture that she may never have. I have access to medications and a pharmacy around the corner. Without PEPFAR money to provide her lifesaving medications, this mother might live only another year and die while her child is still young. With medications, she might live twenty years. She might raise her child. Work. Go to church. Have a life.

Before urging my government to pass PEPFAR, I had never used my voice; I had never lobbied my elected leaders about anything. Lobbying was what special-interest groups did. It was not the job of soccer moms.

Now it rains down on me.

As I stand under the acacia tree outside the hospital, the truth washes over me. I soak in the fact that my advocacy efforts—my voice—matter. I, a stay-at-home American mother, lobbied for the interests of this young Kenyan mom struggling to survive. She doesn't know my name, nor I hers. And we never will.

I am a voice for the voiceless.

■ PRAYER

O heavenly Healer, my heart yearns for a day when all the illnesses of the world will be washed away. Jesus, use me to be a voice for the voiceless, and help me believe my one voice can make a difference. In your name. Amen.

■ WRITING PROMPT

Describe a time when you felt overcome by feelings of inadequacy. What did you do about it, if anything?

I Am a Desperate Woman
by Ashley Hales

I see how each season lies tucked up inside the other. . . . How even the scented explosion of spring lies sleeping within winter branches that seem brittle as death.
—Christie Purifoy, *Roots and Sky*[10]

Most of my breakdowns happen on bathroom floors. When I did not know much about pain, I cried over a wedding-decision standstill, feeling pulled between my identities as daughter and soon-to-be wife. A few years later, when I had the hope of new life within me, I howled, hunched over the toilet as I miscarried my first baby. Since then, I've shut the bathroom door for alone time, hoping to find some inner calm; I've cried on the bathmat when the world felt like it was spinning out of control, when I could no longer be the one to hold together all the loose strands. The bathmat has been my altar—soaked with tears, the vessel to hold my sin, shame, and suffering.

This last October, I cried in the bathroom because I couldn't leave the toilet for more than an hour. I wouldn't stop bleeding. I didn't know what was wrong. My body felt twisted, confused—like it was ridding itself of its life force. This was it, I figured: my body was irreparably broken. I cried for healing, and still the blood came, day after day, hour after hour. How could there be so much? I wrapped myself in workout clothes, layers and layers of clothes, so I could go grocery shopping without looking like a trauma victim, bleeding all over the linoleum floor. I ran to the doctor for tests. I canceled everything—

writing deadlines pushed back, playdates off the calendar—and barely managed feeding my children. There in the bathroom all I could pray was a weak, "Help, God! Please help me!" My voice was plaintive and small. There on the bathmat my voice is always truest. It is there where I whisper my broken hallelujahs.

Truthfully, a desperate "Help!" is not a prayer I've prayed a lot.

I know nothing of suffering. Not really.

I know the stories. Of mothers in Syria being forced to choose which child to take as they flee; of women and girls sold and trafficked; of friends around the globe and in my city who battle chronic and undiagnosed illness; of friends who, because of the color of their skin or the socioeconomic bracket they've been born into, have reason to cry out, "Help!" much more often than I. But me? I'm a suburban mom with a new bleeding problem. I know only a smidgen of suffering.

Yet, my body has deep lessons to teach me. I am learning that this triad of mind, body, and soul is a pretty construct that doesn't hold up. My body exposes where I've chosen to dig down my roots. Often, it turns out, they're in rocky soil.

As a teenager, I first put down roots in two places, one physical, the other mental. I'd dance, tumble, and cheer. I measured my worth by my cheer skirt's waist measurement, by whether I was the best one on top of the cheer stunt, and by whether the boys I liked noticed these things. I also excelled at my honors and advanced-placement classes, realizing that when beauty wore off, when I gained a few pounds, I'd still have my mind. Both body and brains were well-honed machines that I asked to heal me. My soul I put into a compartment of emotional Jesus-y things. I supposed in youth—at least in my sheltered, privileged one—I could keep the boxes of self neat and tidy. Pushing the messiness of life away, I emerged: my voice small, compliant, and always safe and good. It took years to grow into a strong voice of womanhood, one that didn't apologize for taking up bodily and emotional space, one that didn't equate femininity with wearing an invisibility cloak. But as I grew into strength, my soul became fat and lazy, relying on my mental acumen and bodily control.

Now, a different courage is needed. My voice shakes. I eke out a small "Help."

When Jesus is on his way to heal the daughter of Jairus—a prominent religious man who trusted that Jesus could heal his dying girl—Jesus feels power leave him. He stops. In the bustling crowd, he turns around and asks, "Who touched my garments?" (Mk. 5:30 ESV). Everyone is touching him of course; he is in the midst of a crowd. But this touch was different. Power had gone out of him. Not that he didn't know (he is the Son of God), but his question requires the woman to come out of the shadows. When we must vocalize our answer, we muster the courage to name who we really are. This woman isn't supposed to have touched him. She is "unclean," unable to touch any person, let alone this revered rabbi.

But she is desperate. For twelve years she has bled. She has spent her money on doctors who could not heal, on expensive products that did not cure the problem. She has heard reports that Jesus is a healer and thinks, "If I touch even his garments, I will be made well" (Mk. 5:28 ESV). Though she is ostracized from the community, she refuses bitterness. She travels long and far on faith. She reaches out. She touches. She feels the blood stop immediately. Yet, he feels it, too; and now she'll have to tell the truth.

The woman comes forward, trembling. What will Jesus say? The story spills out—the relentless blood, the years and money wasted, the reports of Jesus, the mantra she'd repeated as she made her way to find this holy man. "If I touch even his garments, I will be made well," and she *has* touched and she *is* well. She names her desperation. Instead of seeing her as weak and pathetic, shaming her for her audacity, Jesus calls her "daughter" (Mk. 5:34 ESV). She is grafted into a family that is wider and gentler than she'd expected. Jesus commends her faith and then releases her, stating for the crowd and Jairus (waiting on his own miracle) that her faith has healed her.

But I keep bleeding. My bleeding only slows when I pay for a $100 medication that makes me cry at the price tag. All I have is a plaintive "Help!" cried out to a God whose garment's hem I cannot touch. My prayers and my voice feel weak and ineffectual. The bathroom ceiling feels far away as I'm hunched over on the bathmat. I imagine how much further God must be than the ceiling. I do not yet know what it means that he walks through suffering with us. Instead, I remember what I said to my husband when I was on the edge of sleep a few weeks ago: *God feels distant.* That night, I cried a little and turned over to sleep. Now, the blood still doesn't stop.

I do not know if this bleeding I'm experiencing means hormonal imbalance, or fibroids, or something structurally amiss. What I do know is that I have been stripped bare. My roots are exposed. All my rush and hurry has not saved me. My good mothering days, my writing, my nice Instagram feed, give nothing to me. They are gods that swallow not only my time but also my soul, and they profit me nothing. In the silent moments when I lie down, I'm haunted by a question: What if this blood that doesn't stop is actually God's good?

It strikes me with full force in this week of unstoppable bleeding that maturing is not just a movement up some metaphorical ladder from good to better to best. Part of growing older is coming to terms with our own creatureliness. Our peacock chests will be deflated; as we age, we are growing smaller, weaker, less significant. It's a sobering truth: I am creature, not creator. I will die. It is the broken way of the world that my body and yours will eventually fail. It's shocking when a truth you know in your brain finds its way into your body. If growing up is not simply an upward-slanted line of progress, then growing older and being bent by suffering is not simply a process of increasing degeneration.

Maybe this untethered bleeding is exactly what I need to see my own mortality, to wake up my lazy soul and find my truest voice once again. To regain the still, small voice. Mine is a voice brought low. If this bleeding is how God comes near to me now, then this space where my voice feels weak and unsure is good, too. Now is not the season for shouting. In this fragile replanting, I long to nurture a voice so confident it can even be quiet. What does it look like to nurture quiet strength, to find a home for my voice that reaches beyond circumstances and confidence, where there is abundance and rest?

I repeat and cling to a few words in Exodus, that God is a God "who heals" (Exod. 15:26 NIV). No matter if I feel God or not, if I do or don't sense a still, small voice speaking in my heart or through Scripture, I hold fast to these stories of God as faithful deliverer. I wait on medical answers, but they do not bring me peace that quells anxiety. I wait for healing. I know God is who he says he is, that he is the Great Physician; yet, I hadn't put it together that healing might look entirely different than I imagined. Healing is not something Jesus can *do* for me; it's not a clean bill of health. Healing is, rather, Jesus himself.

Only there on the bathmat do I see myself rightly: I, too, am a desperate woman with nowhere to turn except to a God who calls me "daughter." It is God alone who is immutable, faithful, and perfect. And this bleeding is his good for me. What if this is simply what replanting feels like, with unearthed roots that shiver in the light?

The logic goes the other way: that if you put in your time, effort, and talent, you'll garner success; you put your roots down, and the soil will give you an expected outcome and result. There, you'll flourish: you'll find your purpose, and in so doing, you'll find your voice.

We're told that finding your voice, or building a platform, a ministry, or even a home, means you must shout to be heard. That growing into a calling means bigger and louder. Yet, now, after my week of bleeding, I'm finding the way up is almost always down in God's kingdom. It isn't bigger, louder, better. It is only through our intimate acquaintance with and even affection for grief and suffering that we find out who we are. There, we're called out from the shadows; we're called to lift our faces from the tear-soaked bathmat. Our voices are clearest there, in that small, sheltered space of suffering. Only there is the Gospel good news to us and to others. When we embrace our limitations and our pain, we can birth the sort of vibrant springtime life that the Resurrection promises.

If God is as close to us as clothing,[11] then the "man of sorrows" (Isa. 53:3 ESV) cries out with our suffering and grief, whether that's as we embrace death or as we embrace all the little deaths to self on the way. The Jesus whom the bleeding woman touched cries with me on the toilet. He sees the blood that does not stop. The God of the universe is powerful enough to stop it, but will he? And even if he doesn't, will I only choose to love a God because he does my bidding, because he makes me well? Am I then not making God in my image rather than being conformed to his? I ask each time I have to run to the bathroom to see the blood that keeps coming: *Is his presence here with me in my pain enough? Is God enough?*

I must hope that there is something on the other side of loss. I have no other god, no other story that sees, empathizes, and then promises to redeem my suffering. My voice will only be effective as it is sharpened and shaped through suffering, as I eke out broken hallelujahs. Could it be that it is as gloriously true for our lives as it is for the trees? —when the limbs are bare and all looks lost, curled within is the surprising promise of spring.

■ PRAYER

O Father, you are from everlasting to everlasting. You created galaxies and breathed the breath of life into man and woman. Yet, God, you came to earth as a baby—helpless, needy, and willing to participate in the fallenness of your creation. How often do I run from pain and suffering? Thank you, Jesus, for not doing so. It is only through your embrace of pain and suffering that I have new life. God, show me that no matter my circumstances, you are the prize. Amen.

■ W R I T I N G   P R O M P T

Write a prayer about your broken hallelujahs.

Little Kids, Big Dogs
by Margot Starbuck

I felt my civil rights had been violated and I was fired up.

Incensed, bounding up the south stairwell of Main Street Elementary School toward my first-grade classroom, I schemed how I could expose the egregious injustice. At the tender age of six, I'd already learned that no power-wielding grown-up was going to listen to someone who still had to stand on tippy-toes to reach the water fountain.

During the four-block walk to school, I'd been noodling on the conundrum. By the time I'd reached the octagon-wielding crossing guard at Hill and Main Street, I'd resigned myself to the likely fact that no adult would take the word of a child. Yet, gripping my red metal lunchbox, climbing toward Mrs. Lambert's classroom, the solution fell straight from the heavens.

I would write a book.

Not the stapled eight-pager that so many kindergarteners were pumping out, either. This would be a thick, hard-bound volume, heavy with authority. When I grew up, I'd write the book that would expose the injustice I, and so many others of my ilk, had suffered.

In that divine moment of vocational clarity, I had the odd out-of-body awareness that some other similarly rash six-year-olds would, in the heat of passion, make the same kind of promise—"When I grow up . . . ," they'd threaten—only to forget it the next day.

Not me. Determined, I vowed that decades later I would not forget the suffering of my short weak-armed people. The title of my call to action?

Grown-Ups Think That Little Kids Can't Walk Big Dogs, but They Totally Can.

If I wrote a book, I mused, people would have to listen to me.* (Today, of course, I've discovered that's not the case at all. I've published seven books, and I still can't get a twelve-year-old to pick his socks up off the dining-room floor.)

At six, I experienced this moment of clarity about who I was made to be. There would be others.

Watching my aunt film her young children in the driveway of their Indiana home when I was eight, and swearing that one day I would own a movie camera to document what matters most. Roller-skating in my driveway at nine, deciding I would one day write a book about how to roller-skate.

Giving a winning student-council election speech at Hadley Junior High in Glen Ellyn, Illinois, detailing how being president pro tem was like being a shortstop on a baseball team. Delivering the hard news to my high-school basketball coach that I couldn't play my junior year because I'd be joining the forensics team instead, to perform original monologues in competitions.

Purchasing my first movie camera at nineteen to document a visit to South Africa during the country's apartheid era. Preaching, my twenty-sixth year, while a childhood friend visited our northern New Jersey church and reminded me of the killer student-council speech I'd delivered in seventh grade. Speaking, in my midthirties, at a Wheaton College chapel service, located within walking distance of my grade school and junior high and high school.

Though I couldn't see how the story would unfold—at six, or eight, or sixteen, or twenty-five—I can now look back and recognize the moments when I flourished because I was being exactly who I was made to be.

I hope you can, too.

*Still seeking the right publisher for the dog-walking manifesto.

■ PRAYER

Giver of all good gifts, I long to become all that you made me to be. Guard me from the trap of comparison, that I might become the wonderfully unique human you created me to be for your glory. Amen.

■ WRITING PROMPT

Write about a memory from your childhood or young adulthood when you were flourishing because you were doing what you were made to do.

Finding My Activist Voice
by April Yamasaki

I don't do personality tests. No, I don't know what color I am, what eighties cartoon character I'm most like, or which Star Wars character, which animal, and so on. I've stayed away from the Enneagram even though friends have found it helpful, and I only made an exception for the Myers-Briggs test because my denomination had me take it for professional development.

"Nope," I mutter as I scroll past yet another invitation to take a personality test. Between full-time pastoral ministry, my writing life, and keeping up with family and friends, personality tests remain firmly on my "I don't do" list. They're right up there with mowing the lawn (now that we live in a townhouse), donating money over the telephone (since even with caller ID I can never really know who's calling), and making any recipe with more than a page of instructions (since I love to cook, only not quite *that* much).

At the same time, I reserve the right to make exceptions. After all, what's the use of a self-made rule if you can't unmake it when there seems good reason? So when I received a review copy of *Your Vocational Credo* by Deborah Koehn Loyd,[12] I set aside my list to take her Vocational Preferences survey. How else could I rate its accuracy? How could I review her book without trying her survey for myself?

I dutifully worked my way through her questionnaire:

5. Are you delighted by developing relationships with others or seek to relieve suffering?

16. Do you live as a daredevil or have a visionary and strategic outlook toward life?

33. Are you sometimes accused of being a matchmaker, or do you find value in changing minds?[13]

After these and many other questions, I added up my scores to determine my top three preferences.

Preference 3 turned out to be Communicator. No surprise there. In my current pastoral work focused on preaching, teaching, and pastoral care, and in my writing that includes both blogging and book writing, I spend a lot of time communicating, and I love it! Preference 2 added up to Organizer, and that seemed to fit also. I make lists. I like to organize my work at the end of the day so I can return to it fresh in the morning. So far, so good—the Vocational Preferences survey seemed to mirror my vocational preferences in real life.

Until I got to Preference 1: Activist. Yes, I like to get things done, but really, *Activist?* As a pastor, I'm often a catalyst for new ministry, from planting a Vietnamese church to starting a Green Team on creation care to hiring new staff. More personally, when my mother was still alive, I consistently advocated for her care, at home and in the hospital. I saw myself as a communicator and organizer, a catalyst and advocate. But an activist? I wasn't so sure.

And then my husband abruptly lost his job.

After twenty-five years of teaching at a small Christian college, with a spotless record, and more academic publishing credits than any other faculty member, my husband received the devastating news that his employment would be terminated—not through any fault of his own, but due to college finances. Such news would have been painful at any time, but the notice came just two-and-a-half weeks before Christmas, just three weeks before his major book-publishing deadline, with end-of-semester marking still to come. What's more, the college administration expected him to teach until the end of the

next semester, had already hired a younger professor to take over the
following year, and wanted him to say nothing about the termination
outside of his immediate family and professional advisers. It felt like a
death in the family, only without being able to mourn properly.

I lamented the loss of my husband's job, but even more I lamented
the loss of his confidence and joy in ministry. I lamented that the college
was no longer the people and place we thought it had been—not a family
of good relationships, but a place of disrespect and brokenness. I lamented
the loss of staff morale as others wondered if they would be next—perhaps
not this Christmas, but some other time, maybe when they would be
turning sixty. I lamented the loss for students, for our denomination as
part owner of the college, and for the community at large.

"Does the administration know what they're doing?" asked one
student leader. "Your husband brings credibility to the whole program."

"How could they do this?" asked a professor at another institution.
"The scholars I know in their sixties and seventies are doing their best
work."

"They've made a terrible mistake and should apologize," said a
local pastor, "but do they have the strength to do that?"

As my husband's situation became known in the community, I
began hearing more stories of employment difficulties with other
Christian organizations and churches, both within and beyond our
denomination. A friend of a friend didn't even realize that her job in a
Christian institution was ending, and her replacement already hired—
until she heard the announcement at the annual staff Christmas party.
Another friend received her termination notice from a Christian
organization during a round of budget cuts—let go immediately and
without warning while away from the office, her passwords suddenly
changed, with no opportunity that day to pick up her personal
belongings or say good-bye to coworkers.

As a way of coping with our personal distress, I had been journaling
privately about the experience, but as I heard these and other stories, I

realized that my husband and I were not alone. Many others experienced painful church employment practices around terminations, hiring, handling grievances, staff reviews, and more. With dismay, I learned that some of the "retirements" I had heard about over the last few years had not been retirements at all, but painful terminations without cause and with little or no accountability for leadership.

Instead of accepting it and walking away quietly, my husband chose to remain connected and work for positive change. The college president eventually apologized for giving him notice during the Christmas season. The college board agreed to review my husband's recommendations, which included the college respecting all human rights provisions, including protection against discrimination for race and gender *and* age. The accrediting body that oversees the college required that it develop a clear grievance procedure, as well as a faculty handbook clarifying policies and procedures. While these things have yet to be fully realized, at least they remain the subject of conversation and further process.

Yet what of those in similar circumstances who do not have my husband's legal background? Who may feel they have no choice but to remain silent about their experience? Who may not know what questions to ask around leadership, ethics, and accountability? Who may not have the persistence to work for institutional change and follow through? It takes enormous energy to be the lone voice in the wilderness crying for change, especially when dealing with your own emotional upheaval and the need to find alternative employment to support yourself and your family.

That's why I decided to start writing publicly on church employment with a new blog: *When You Work for the Church: The Good, the Bad, and the Ugly, and How We Can All Do Better*. I'm certainly no expert, but I'm learning a lot and want to share it to support others, to help the church and other Christian organizations do better in employment matters. I think we *want* to do better as brothers and sisters in Christ, in keeping with God's call to live with integrity and justice, loving God and loving one another. Even if employment relationships need to change, we're still brothers and sisters in the same church, and need to treat one another with respect.

To that end, I've blogged about my husband's journey from disbelief to constructive response in the difficult loss of his employment. I've shared what I'm learning about how to survive in the aftermath of painful job termination, how to write a job description, and how to be an effective board member. I'm finding others who write on similar themes, and working at amplifying those voices that can help the church and other Christian organizations do better, both as employers and employees.

That Vocational Preferences survey got it right after all. I've become an activist in my own modest way. I say "modest" because I'm not out picketing and because the need for better church employment practice may not seem as dire as eliminating sex trafficking or systemic racism. Yet poorly handled personnel situations have far-reaching effects. Some abruptly terminated employees go to a different church or denomination, or leave ministry entirely. Some come close to suicide and struggle with depression and anxiety. All this impacts the spouse and children, who must live with the disruption and stress, who may even become estranged from God and the church. The church or other Christian organizations may suffer a loss of confidence in leadership, a loss of morale among employees, a loss of reputation in the wider community, a loss of Christian witness. Ministry suffers. The kingdom of God suffers.

Your Vocational Credo defines an activist as one who seeks to make things right, who asks, "Why isn't someone doing something about this?"[14] I'm raising that question around church employment. Why do churches and other Christian organizations seem to handle employee relationships so poorly? Or do Christian employees have unreasonable expectations of their employers? Why do apparently good, well-meaning Christian people seem to struggle on both sides of the employer-employee relationship, and what can we do about this? Through painful personal experience, by God's grace, and in community with others, I'm branching out and growing into my activist voice.

You may not identify yourself as an activist any more than I did, but God has given you unique experiences, preferences, pains, and passions. And you, too, can grow into them as expressions of your faith and hope in God. Where is that place of pain in your life, where God consoles you with a consolation that can bless and console others? (2 Cor. 1:3–11). Where do you find joy and passion for living that can encourage and spur others "to love and good deeds"? (Heb. 10:24 NASB).

As we continue to branch out in the riches of God's grace, may we attend to the Lord's ongoing work in our lives. May we hear the voice of Jesus calling. May we be filled, transformed, and empowered by the Holy Spirit as we respond.

■ PRAYER

O God of love and justice, you long to make things right. I confess that I am often the problem as I labor under the weight of sin. By your grace, forgive and redeem me. Receive my unique experiences, preferences, pains, and passions, and use them to make a positive difference in your world. Amen.

■ WRITING PROMPT

Where is that place of pain in your life, where God consoles you with a consolation that can bless and be a voice for others?

Red Lips, Holy Rebellion, and Lady Danger
by Alia Joy

Oh, honey, you are much too yellow-complected for red, plus red draws attention to your teeth. I always tell my customers to work with what they've got. For you Orientals, I always say stick with your eyes, they're so . . . exotic." She purses her lips at me, her fuchsia lipstick bleeding into the tiny wrinkles along her mouth. She tells me which parts are worthy of being seen and which parts aren't.

I leave the makeup counter with mascara. I spend my twenties wearing colorless ChapStick and lip balm because my teeth don't line up white and brilliant. I don't line up white and brilliant. I learn to smile with my mouth pressed shut.

When I was a girl, I had never seen an Asian American model. There were no shows featuring prominent Asian American actors. There were hardly any books about Asian American characters. Our leaders were white, our television shows were white, our neighborhood was white. To be white was to belong, to be beautiful, to be someone who could smile with her whole mouth and open it and be heard. But I was just a girl. I hadn't yet learned that I could own my story, that it could help me become someone.

When I entered my classrooms in grade school, I was greeted by rooms full of white faces. Lunch boxes with Jem and the Holograms or Transformers lined the shelf above the hooks where we hung our coats. Kids begged their moms for Lunchables, and when we went to the Skaggs Alpha Beta supermarket, I asked for the cardboard boxes of waxy cheese, crackers, and a small stack of clammy ham, too.

I didn't want to be the girl whose house always had a rice pot plugged in on the counter, whose pantry was filled with seaweed and saimin noodles and Spam, whose fridge smelled of kimchee when you opened it. My taste buds never understood why the tiny stacks in the Lunchables box were anything to be desired, beyond being a way for me to line up on the shelf right next to my peers. I wanted to fit in, to belong, to be seen.

As much as I longed to be the same, with blonde hair and blue eyes, and a name like Jennifer or Sarah, I wasn't. Even well-meaning teachers saw me as other. In an effort to recognize my "roots," one such teacher pulled me aside after class to offer me some guidance.

"You might like to do your project on Connie Chung," she offered, smiling down at me, her hand placed gently on my shoulder. "Yes, I think that'd be a perfect fit for you, Alia."

And that night I sat at our kitchen table swinging my legs that had yet to grow enough to touch the ground. I labeled my paper, Alia Boston, grade 3, and then wrote in perfect letters across the top "Someone I Admire" with a sharpened number-two pencil, and then I asked my mom who Connie Chung was. It was only when I stood in front of the class to give my presentation to a sea of white faces and blonde hair with every blue eye on me that I realized everyone else got to pick Michael Jordan or Ronald Reagan or Molly Ringwald. I was assigned someone.

I was an Asian American girl in a white world. No matter where I was, I could only be seen one way. The same. Asian Americans are seen as the same. It didn't matter that I had no idea who Connie Chung was or that I am not Chinese American; it only mattered that she was our mascot, patron saint of Asian kids. Later, I would add Kristi Yamaguchi and Michelle Kwan even though I never cared a thing about figure skating.

Unfortunately, Asian Americans get so few opportunities for representation in our culture that we are forced to cling to the few we have whether we like them or not.

The normative experience, the default, the factory setting, is white. With whiteness, there is no danger of a single story, because white is seen as varied and nuanced and individual. We who are not white experience the limitations of a single story. White people get to be whole individuals.

At a blogging conference a few years ago, I realized not much has changed since I was a girl. I was there for three days and was constantly meeting new people. I never got my childhood wish of being called Jennifer or Sarah, so my name is distinct. There aren't a lot of other women my age named Alia.

At the beginning of the conference, I pick up my welcome packet with my name printed neatly in black letters, and yet for the next three days I am called Dawn.

"No, it's Alia, actually," I say pointing to my lanyard once again. We make small talk, and they keep referencing things I know nothing about. I try to figure out why people I've just met keep calling me Dawn. This is the third time.

I see her on the last day of the blogging conference; she's easy to spot because she sticks out, too. She's at least three inches taller than me with a short, efficient brown bob to my long black hair. I've got a good eighty pounds on her. And there it is on her lanyard: Dawn. She's Asian American, too.

I've felt it my whole life. It's the playground where they would pull their eyes into a grotesque slant and chant, "Ching chong China girl," at me. It's the woman at the makeup counter telling me what is not beautiful about me. It's a thousand other times when a stereotype sufficed for the whole of me, and I slinked away unseen or uninvited.

I'm the girl who listened to New Kids on the Block and loved Jonathan just like all the other girls in her class. I am the girl who wrote her report on Connie Chung and believed red lipstick was off-limits for her. I am the girl who followed makeup tutorials in *Seventeen* magazine and tried to make all the blended shadow fit my tiny crease of eyelid. There was only one brand of beauty. She had a jaw like cut marble, smooth and long as a pedestal, and when she smiled the pearls danced in her mouth, white teeth lined up and brilliant in a face of milky porcelain or dusty beige. She had four shades of blue eyeshadow on her lids and space for more. She was tall and willowy with just enough curve, and she floated when she walked. Her teased hair could be brown or blonde or red or black, but not her skin. She was white and brilliant.

But I am not a girl anymore.

These days I eat saimin piled with kimchee, and I am irked that kimchee, the smell of which made my face go red as a girl when friends came over and plugged their noses and gagged at my fridge, is now being sold at Costco to hipsters and soccer moms in yoga pants.

These days I don't listen to the women at the makeup counter. I choose my color. MAC makes my favorite red lipstick. I twist it from the bullet, and it rises up in brazen scarlet and smears across my lips. Lady Danger on my lips is holy rebellion. I smack them together and lean into the mirror. I see all of me. I am a biracial Asian American woman, and I am beautiful; I am worthy of being seen. The strength to believe it is something I fight for every day. These lips were created to speak truth.

I've got fire on my lips, blazing red. This holy rebellion says, *I will be seen.* I'm learning to harness my voice even when it strangles in my throat, because these things need saying.

For all the progress we've made, we haven't gotten that far. One only need flip on the TV to see that although we have more Asians on the screen, and in the movies, too, they are still bound to single stories: the ninja, the tech guy, the tiger mom's prodigy, the geisha/seductress, and the wise old master, to name a few. We're still not seen as fully human, nuanced, and dimensional.

I knew the Oscar nominations were predominantly white—Twitter tossed around #Oscarssowhite for months. I watched Chris Rock trot out three Asian kids and make a tired joke at their expense. People laughed, and I wanted to rage and collapse onto the floor and weep. I was glad I had sent my daughter to bed during the ballgown entrance of the stars. An Asian woman hasn't won an Oscar in fifty-eight years. More white women have played Asians than actual Asians. People of color are absent or woefully underrepresented in almost every sphere of North American life. The Oscars just happened to have a hashtag.

A woman of color is fully human, not just a sidekick, a caricature, or a stereotype. The world chooses not to see me when I'm omitted from the lineup, from the role, from the stage, from the country, the page, or the screen.

These days, I say we need more stories written by women who are not just white and brilliant. I'm erased when you don't recognize my brand of beautiful, whatever that may be—when all the standard samples from Sephora are creamy nude, but nude only means white. I am silenced when you say, "It's just a movie awards show; it's no big deal. Why do you even care?" When the Oscar's whiteness has much less to do with a golden statue than it does with the idol of white supremacy.

You say, "How will we have unity if you keep bringing up race?" I say, your unity looks to me like uniformity, and we cannot grow when we make art that believes a single story or race or skin type has more merit than another. We cannot create when we cannot even see clearly. That kind of art is reductive, not expansive; it drives us further away from our humanity instead of closer to it.

Because we shouldn't have to decide between being known and being loved. As children of the God who sees, we get both. We all get to be seen if for no other reason than that God looks on with eyes of adoration and has never been about the single, dominant story.

God is not about the status quo or business as usual. God is the one who disrupts, who intervenes, who delivers. God is for the oppressed, for the marginalized, for the refugee, for the captives, for the sick, for the other. God is for the ones the world's gaze skims over, the ones who never belong or get invited.

God is about holy imagination and believing for better things. We must be people who choose to see if we want to be like Jesus. So I'm begging you to pay attention so we're not all called Dawn. Women of color need to be on main stages with mics to drop when they faithfully show up and say the hard and necessary things.

Omission is oppression of the cruelest kind. You erase me when you omit me, but I have a right to be here and to be seen and to be known because God sent Jesus—giving all people not only the nomination but the invitation to belong.

We need to be in your homes and on your screens. We need to have stories in your bookstores and voices behind your microphones so my daughter will have a greater choice for her "Someone I Admire" project, and so will yours. Because only then will we begin to see the beauty intended in the body's reflection, the *imago Dei* made brilliant and colorful. Only then will we recognize the truth of who we are, seen and loved, belonging to each other.

So I speak in holy rebellion, against the blindness to which we are all prone, in lips baptized by Lady Danger.

■ PRAYER

Lord, help us be women who see past the burden of small imagination and reductive thinking, and lead us into your redemptive dream for the world. Help us see each other fully in the ways we are diverse and the ways we are unified. Let us not grow weary in seeking the good of our neighbor; let us not grow toward pride, but humble us in your truth. Let us love as you love, speak as you call, and honor the image of God in all our brothers and sisters. Let us be one as you are one. Amen.

■ WRITING PROMPT

Describe your holy rebellion, or what you dream it would look like.

The Motherless Mother
by Adelle Gabrielson

The day Colin, our first child, was born, my husband, Gabe, was at my side. My father and mother-in-law were in the waiting room. My mom, suffering from a hereditary, neurodegenerative illness called Huntington's disease, was living four hundred miles away on Catalina Island. Apart from us all, in the contrived contentedness she had manufactured for herself there, she was happy. She didn't want to leave the island. That was the best we could get from her, and so we left it at that. The spot I had always imagined she would take, by my side throughout my pregnancy, doting over my growing belly, at every baby shower, sat empty. I trudged through my pregnancy, elated and exhausted, and every day missing my mommy.

Huntington's has been called the most devastating disease known to humankind. Imagine being in your forties and having Parkinson's, Alzheimer's, and ALS at the same time. Some patients are fortunate to experience primarily physical degeneration with some dementia. Others, like my mother, suffer cruelly from mental illness—paranoia, schizophrenia—while also enduring the spasmodic muscle contractions called chorea, which has twisted her face and hands, and constantly affects her balance and ability to walk. Because it is a hereditary illness, most patients watched their own parents suffer first, living in fear of their own possible future. A 50/50 chance, the toss of a coin, is all that lies between life and Huntington's.

As I lay in recovery after a C-section, attended only by a disinterested nurse, I slipped under the surface of grief and drowned in it for a while. Why isn't she here? My husband stood vigil with our baby as they checked him over from stem to stern, head, shoulders, knees, and toes. And here I was, completely alone on what was supposed to be the most joyous day of my life, gasping for what I had lost. The void of her presence, dark and yawning, drained the room of light and life. I wept violently, the pain excruciating.

The nurse never even raised her head.

Throughout my childhood, I had known of the great family evil that lurked in our DNA. I knew that my grandmother was not as she once was. She hobbled and bobbed, unable to drive, her arms waving about in the gruesome chorea that typifies the disease. My mother, back then, would not speak of this family illness. My father told me to pray. And pray I did. I prayed that God would spare my mom, spare her the indignity and disability her mother had suffered. The incontinence and convalescence. The forced withdrawal to continuous care and lack of independence. I prayed in faith. I prayed in confidence. I believed, believed to my core, that she would be spared. The faith of a child.

But God said no.

Slowly, subtly, the illness began to take over my mother's life and rob her of the person she was and the person she could have been. Once gentle and kind, she became angry and paranoid. Convinced of a family-wide conspiracy, she demanded to remove herself from our daily lives and took up residence in the tiny town of Avalon on Catalina Island, thirty miles off the coast of Long Beach. She was safe there, could walk to wherever she needed, and we accepted that this was the best she could give.

We spoke on the phone from time to time. We'd talk of Catalina and the weather. She'd tell me of the people she would meet and the friends she would make. But we would never talk about why she was there and we were here and all that was so wrong, so broken. She would merrily say good-bye as if a loving wife and mother moving to an island to escape the reality of her illness and family were a perfectly normal thing.

～⌒～

As my husband and I set about being a family of two adults and one child, I realized quickly that two plus one does not actually equal three. The sum is exponentially more than the individual parts. I couldn't stop to think about how different this was from the way I envisioned it long ago. Noticeably absent, of course, was my mother. She wasn't there by my side to show me tips and tricks she had learned as a mother herself. She wasn't there to lend an extra pair of hands. She wasn't there to rock the baby while I napped for twenty minutes. She wasn't there to marvel at the new gadgets and baby gear, astonished that she had been able to survive motherhood without a video baby monitor and a Boppy.

She wasn't there.

Within a week of my son's birth, we were alone, figuring it all out for ourselves. We named him Colin, and he was downy and precious. But like every infant, the boy had lungs and used them. Postpartum insomnia, something the books failed to mention but a very real and not-so-terribly uncommon manifestation of postpartum depression, set in. "Sleep when the baby sleeps!" the old ladies at church would tell me cheerfully, patting my cheek. I wanted to punch one of them. The baby slept fine. He was a dream, really. He quickly adopted a schedule and woke with sunshine on his face. But for me, sleeping became a demon I dreaded. Trying to sleep and failing was an exhausting, humiliating battle.

It took me a month to call my doctor, so disillusioned with myself that I felt like a complete failure. Failure at breastfeeding, failure at sleep. She prescribed sleeping medication, told my husband that he was now on duty for the 11:00 PM feeding, and sent me to bed at eight o'clock.

I woke the next day at six and immediately began to cry with relief. If you had told me when Colin was just two weeks old that I would, someday, sleep ten straight hours, I would have told you that you were lying, and I might have kicked you in the shins.

Too tired, too worried, too lost, I could not stop to think about my mom. Remembering was too painful, the scab of her absence too fresh. Memories plucked at the wound, and before long it bled; I simply did not have time between diapers and formula and breastfeeding to be able to process that kind of pain. She was not here. What was evident was the void she should have filled, a gaping black hole that took everything with it, including the light. My loss became a veil through which I saw the world, tinged and tainted by my grief.

God said no. My faith was shattered. My prayers—they were pure and righteous and faithful. If a faith of a mustard seed can move a mountain, surely mine could spare one person a slow and painful illness and early death.

But God said no.

Disappointment, they say, is the delta between expectations and reality.

My disappointment was a chasm—deep, wide, dark, and cold—into which I fell and believed I would never find my way out.

As I carefully tried to adapt to the new role of motherhood without a mother of my own to call upon, I convinced myself that I had been raised by the perfect mom, and therefore, I had to be the perfect mom. Never yell. Never cry. Never fight. Never make mistakes. Never apologize. I focused only on her serenity, the ease with which she had mothered us. Motherhood, to my surprise, was not easy, and I wasn't adapting well. Frantic to live up to the ideal I manufactured, I found myself alone and shivering, in the shadow of the pedestal I had placed her on. Nothing was easy; nothing came naturally to me, except perhaps anxiety, fear, and worry.

I was exceptionally good with all of those.

When Colin was three months old, I joined the ranks of working mothers and returned on a limited schedule as director of client services for a Silicon Valley advertising firm. I juggled the guilt of leaving my newborn in day care and the heady rush of wearing makeup and heels again. I loved the dichotomy. Whatever the day brought, the next day would be different. If clients were demanding and critical, the next day would be spent in yoga pants nuzzling the sweet-smelling neck of my boy. If he was fussy and colicky all day, the next day would bring silence and solitude as I drove to work and played with grown-ups instead of Baby Einstein.

I was unable to ask for help. I did not know I had permission to do so. I thought I was supposed to have all the answers the day I delivered my son. Somehow, I never was able to find the manual the stork should have brought. Lack of sleep, rocking a feverish baby at midnight, tap-dancing through client meetings and calls from day care—no one else was struggling with this . . . were they?

Colin, fair-skinned and rosy, with pale blue eyes, began developing strange rashes on his face and legs. They would bloom rapidly, from nothing into a scaly, angry rash that covered his face within hours. The day care would call, certain he had developed some horrifying communicable disease. I would drop work and race to pick him up. The doctor would assure me it was benign and harmless—eczema. "He has sensitive skin," we were told.

Meanwhile, our cherub walked around with a frightening scaly rash covering half his face. I felt responsible. Why couldn't I stop it? We limited his diet and pursued allergy testing. I sat in sterile waiting rooms while he, wearing nothing but a diaper, sat on my lap watching cartoons after two dozen tiny needles full of allergens had been pressed into the petal-soft skin of his little back. All negative.

Deep down, in the dark place bitterness dwells, I squirmed with conviction: *If Mom were here, none of this would have ever happened.*

Mom's illness progressed to the point of required incarceration in a convalescent home when Colin was three years old. She lived there another year, barely lucid, physically incapacitated. We tried to visit, tried to find normalcy as we wheeled her into the sunshine one Mother's Day so she could watch her grandchildren playing on the steps outside. But she wasn't there. Long gone, robbed of life and capability by her illness.

Mom died suddenly of a heart attack, and it became official. I no longer had to explain away the absence of a parent who was still alive but not. When someone loses their spouse, they become a widow or widower. What is a child who loses a parent? There is no word— perhaps because it is simply too big, too massive, to contain in a single word.

Milestones are when I miss her most. I have a mom-shaped hole. A place that will never heal, never close over. It will always be there, and she will always be missing, and there is simply no way around it. What aches is the spot she would have held. I have learned to expect the pain and the regret that is always and forever married to every milestone of my life.

The day I met Pat, I was almost offended by her audacity. New to the area, a mother of grown boys and a hopeful future grandma, she approached me at a church event. She complimented me on my young son. Affronted that this woman, a total stranger, would approach me despite my carefully positioned cloak of bitterness, I responded to her questions with chilly reserve.

 She didn't seem to notice, and within days she had swept me into an embrace of friendship and affection. I slowly thawed in the warmth of her kindness and, over time, allowed her to shower our small family with the motherly love for which I had so long been starving. We became Lucy and Ethel; she offered me the tips and tricks she had learned raising her own three boys, and a willing pair of hands to help and hold and diaper. She was part of our lives for just three years, but in that time my broken heart began to beat again. She helped me find the courage and confidence my mothering desperately lacked, and when I failed, she helped me forgive myself for not being perfect and find the humor in it all. When she moved to be closer to her own sons and soon-to-arrive grandchildren, other women slipped into the space her warmth had thawed.

I now see that the darkness into which I so deeply submerged myself was not so dark after all. Though I was unable to ask for help, help was offered to me anyway, and often. I did not always accept, but sometimes—like with Pat—I wasn't given the choice. God allowed my mother to be removed from this earth, but he also provided women who pushed into my life, despite my chilly exterior—who saw through my pride. Women who supplied the counsel and comfort, assurance and levity, I desperately longed for.

Years pass. Our second son, Michael, is born, and I have time to find my own balance as a mother. I've discovered that while I cannot simply call Mom for answers, there are many women in my life I can call upon. I have learned to trust myself and not the impossible standards I manufactured in my head. I've learned to stop comparing my choices with those of other mothers.

Mother does know best—and that mother is *me*.

■ PRAYER

Father, for all the times you supplied my needs before I cried out for help; for all the moments you provided and I was too blind to see the source; for all the ways you comforted my anguish when I failed to ask; for all the prayers unspoken, but still heard—thank you. Amen.

■ WRITING PROMPT

Reflect on your own ideas of motherhood using this statement: Mother knows best.

Bringing Home Peace
by Ruth Bell Olsson

She folded her hands in her lap as she leaned forward and proposed,
"Perhaps he is not a distraction from your contemplation,
but rather an instrument of your contemplation?"

As the leaves changed and dropped from the trees in the fall of 2011, my life changed and dropped out from underneath me, too. My skin was burning with an outrageous case of poison ivy, we bought a car from a man who lied about its condition, my father became gravely ill with a rogue illness that could not be identified, a key relationship unraveled and tangled, and the dishwasher broke. With every dirty cup or spoon that accumulated in the sink, I could feel my blood pressure rise. I shook with anger and grief over all of the ways in which my life was untenable.

These negative circumstances were piled right on top of an already excruciating seven-year stretch of waiting. Waiting for an answered prayer, waiting for a child.

As an HIV/AIDS activist at the start of this millennium, I traveled to South Africa to see firsthand the devastation left in the wake of the virus. I already knew the statistics, and I could speak movingly about the trajectory of this horrific illness. Yet, it is one thing to read about a monumental, global catastrophe and quite another to encounter it face-to-face. I sat in clinics with dying women, I met with health-care workers who remained steadfastly committed to work that never abated, and I met children. The orphan rate in South Africa alone is in the millions—literally millions of children abandoned or being raised by siblings. On that first trip, as our American team disembarked from the van in a rural area outside of Johannesburg, we were mobbed by bright smiles and tiny waving hands. A sea of little ones. "Where are their parents?" I asked our host. "Dead," was his blunt response. This was a reality I could not wrap my mind or heart around. I didn't even try.

I returned from that trip feeling the weight of a thousand children on my back. They were with me in my dreams and with me every time I gave a speech or wrote an article. My husband and I decided that we had room in our home and room in our family for more children. Perhaps this was the next right step?

Since South Africa and the United States have no adoption agreement, we were told no at every turn. On my many subsequent trips to Johannesburg and Cape Town, I was repeatedly persuaded that there was no adoption path for us. This did not sit well with my soul.

We contacted a lawyer, we joined random circles of adoption advocates, we attempted a home study, we prayed, we complained, we lost hope, and then we resurrected it. It was exhausting.

Halfway through our seven-year journey, a local adoption provider gave us a glimmer of hope that laws were changing. We began yet another process of paperwork and meetings. I would find myself driving around in what felt like interminable circles with pieces of paper that had to be notarized and *apostilled*, and letters that had to be composed precisely—I took endless fingerprints and wrote endless checks. I felt like Sisyphus pushing an adoption rock up an impossible hill, never to reach our son or daughter at the top. Was this simply an exercise in futility? Was this an angry joke by a cruel God testing us to see if we would follow him even if we never got what we wanted? I would pound the steering wheel and yell at God, "How is this helping? How are these ridiculous pieces of paper leading us to a child? Do you even notice that millions of children are languishing in and out of orphanages while we have a warm and waiting home?"

I grew tired of my rants, and probably God did, too. I settled into a low-grade despair that provided the subtext to my life. Maybe God cared, but maybe God didn't. I wasn't sure. When all hell broke loose that notorious fall, my suspicions about God's care for us deepened. It is one thing to wait seven years for a prayer to be answered—this is a model ribboned throughout Scripture—but to wait *and* have calamity strike on multiple fronts? Well, that is just plain mean.

I began to seriously question God's goodness. Perhaps there is a limit to what God can or will do. Where exactly was God in all of this?

As fall began to transition into winter that year, we took a trip. We bundled up my fragile father and headed to warm weather for a bit of recuperation. Amid the compounding stresses of our daily lives, we were the walking wounded, and what should have been a vacation looked more like an ICU postemergency.

It was there in our hotel room that the call came. My cell phone jangled on the dresser top, and I hesitated. *No more bad news. I can't take it.* I let it ring a few more times before slowly picking it up. "Hello?" Our social worker's high and squeaky voice rushed through the line, and she could hardly speak fast enough. "It is a boy, two years and nine months, healthy. . . . You have two weeks to decide if you want him. . . ." She was practically giddy as she relayed details that I did not have the capacity to absorb.

I hung up the phone and turned toward my husband and began to sob. "I can't do this. Not now. This is too much. What are we going to do?"

Then I turned toward God and in anger questioned, "*Now? Seriously, now?* When our whole world feels like it is falling apart, you choose *now*?" The timing of this call felt like the cosmic joke of a punishing God. I knew that this road of adoption would not necessarily be easy. This little boy could have major issues that would need strong and healthy parents able to step up. Could I be that parent? Could I help a child when I was the one gasping for air, barely above water? I was drowning in my own grief and questions. At a time when I knew I would need to be strong, I could not have felt weaker.

Back home a few days later, I slowly read through all the paperwork our social worker had sent. We were drinking in the details of this little boy's life and wondering if we would be his future family. I sat at my desk and decided to look up the meaning of his name. I knew my African friends' names all held deep significance and often shaped their identity and carriage, and I wondered what mantle this little boy had been given.

I stared at the computer screen in disbelief. What I needed so deeply and desperately was right in front of me: *peace*. My son's name means peace.

The exact thing I was hollering and bellowing about was what God was offering to me in the form of a son. An overwhelming sense of the Spirit surrounded me in my tiny office and spoke directly to my heart to reassure me that, no, God is not mean. God does not have ill intentions for me. God is not indifferent.

Instead, God is with me, in all of the pain of the last seven years. The numerous times my fists curled toward heaven or hammered the dash of my car, God was there. In all of the illness, fractured relationships, loss, and worry of the past many months, God had held me. Instead of offering me more misery, God had a plan of blessing. God had a son waiting to be my messenger of peace. This son was a constant reminder that God is the Prince of Peace, the author of peace, and the perfecter of peace.

That winter we moved to South Africa for a season to finalize our son's adoption. This was not an easy journey; there were major complications, many of which involved my physical health. Plus, the idea that God would send me a messenger of peace in the form of a three-year-old boy is hilarious. My son "Peace" is a rambunctious, lively child. He was very attached to me right away and would climb on me like a human jungle gym. He would sometimes bite us or scratch us— almost as if he needed to solidify our physical presence. He is verbal and sassy and knew all kinds of words from the orphanage that made our older children giggle. Yet, I knew I had something to learn about the God of peace from this little person. I never questioned that he was the boy God intended for me.

Clearly he is just a boy and not some kind of angel, but, like all of us, he carries the divine spark. He is a being created in the image and likeness of God. As a mother of three, I will attest that each of my children is a gift. They teach me every day about life, love, and hope. But this little one was sent on a heavenly errand. The timing of his arrival was meant for me. That day I sat and stared at the computer screen reading the definition and origins of his name, I knew. I just knew. In my fear and frustration and my inability to live in the moment and see joy, God was going to use this child to open my heart in a new way.

Months after our transition back to the States, we were all doing well. The car was running fine, and we had a new, beautiful dishwasher. Yet, I found myself frustrated. I felt distant from God. How could I spend time with God—praying and listening—while caring for this active child? I took this question to my spiritual director and complained about how I was having trouble being a truly contemplative Christian. I mentioned that my new son is very busy and opinionated. I love this about him, but I am struggling with how to grow deeper in my faith when I keep getting distracted.

"Perhaps," she said, "this precious child is not a distraction from your contemplation, but rather *an instrument of your contemplation?*"

Contemplation is often defined as meditation, sometimes as thinking about spiritual things. In contemplative prayer, we move beyond words to the mystery of knowing God. This does not happen in a vacuum. I was attempting to remove myself from my life as a devotion to God, yet my spiritual director was proposing the opposite: bringing the gift of contemplative listening right into the ordinary moments of the day. The peace I so desperately crave is being constantly offered to me—in the everyday moments of my life. My son, as my messenger of peace, is that reminder. I knew this, but I had lost the vision of what it could mean. I was missing the concept that perhaps God gave me my son as a way to see and experience the divine. Maybe through the eyes of a happy child who lives *in the moment* I can see God more clearly? Ah, to live with a constant sense of holy wonder. This is the way of peace.

▨ PRAYER

Lord, may we be people who seek your peace. May we live with active contemplation of your mystery and provision. Amen.

▨ WRITING PROMPT

Describe an encounter with a messenger of peace.

Passover, Betrayal, and Deep Redemption
by Catherine McNiel

She leans over to pass the plate of bitter herbs, her shawl grazing the edge of the Passover table. The bitterness is to remind us of our bondage, our suffering. And my phone rings.

Reaching down to silence the ringer, I recognize the name of a neighbor I hardly know, rarely talk to, and never call. I ignore it.

"Why on this night do we dip the herbs twice?" My child asks the traditional question, and our host offers the traditional answer: The greenness of the herbs reminds us of springtime, of new life. We dip the parsley in salt to remember the weeping. We dip the bitter herbs in sweetness to recall that from suffering comes redemption.

And my phone rings again.

Around the table we drink a cup of wine, symbolizing deliverance—and my phone rings.

We cover and uncover the matzah, a picture of brokenness and division that will one day become wholeness and unity—and my phone rings.

Finally, I am alarmed enough to excuse myself and step into the next room. As the rituals of suffering-becoming-redemption are carried out around me, I struggle to absorb the news from my frantic neighbor: I have been the victim of a crime. During the reenacting of this Passover I am pulled away—away from this same reenactment that Judas hastily left so many years ago. He left this ceremony of suffering and hope to betray. I am pulled away to discover that I am betrayed.

All through the long dark night my husband and I search for understanding. Silent car rides, meetings with police, confrontations with the accused. We stand outdoors in the cold, looking through windows—our windows—from the outside. Standing in darkness, peering into a dimly lit room, wondering how to get from where we are back into the light.

We had moved recently, and our condo, our first home, was under contract to be sold. Everything about this change was outside my comfort zone. The market was poor, and the financial hit was staggering. The process moved forward on a knife's edge. And then, just weeks before closing, on Passover, came the unbelievable news that someone we knew had broken into our now-empty home, moved herself in, replaced the locks, drawn up a forged lease, and called it her own.

Amazingly, the law was not on our side; at least not at first. Squatter laws—written with vulnerable women and children in mind—give rights to whoever lives on a property currently, however shaky their legal right to be there. The same laws that offer dearly needed justice to unwanted ex-girlfriends tossed out on the streets by their home-owning boyfriends now put us in an impossible position. The police believed us, but they could not remove the woman and her children from our house. The expertly forged lease she waved in their faces gave them reason even to doubt our story.

For days we held vigil, one of us outside our condo, the other at the police station. For a week, this went on day and night.

It was Holy Week.

Our vigil kept us from marking the sacred days: Palm Sunday, Maundy Thursday, Good Friday, Holy Saturday. But the liturgy and its meaning are written so deeply into my soul that the words echoed through my mind all the same.

So it happened that while I reflected on Holy Week and the alchemy of redemption in Christ—in whom death, sin, pain, suffering, injustice, forgiveness, and love are mingled—in the same physical and mental space, I suffered pain and searing anger, strained for justice, encountered injustice, and longed to be known and vindicated, to forgive and be forgiven, to love and be loved.

Above all, I pondered redemption.

Late at night on Friday, Good Friday, we received a call from the police. New information had been uncovered, and the woman who stole our house had been arrested on other charges, and her children removed. While we still could not legally clear out her things, have keys made, or take back our condo (it would require her voluntary change of heart or a sheriff with a judge's eviction notice to do that), the police let us in to sort out our own belongings.

What a poignant and painful thing it was to walk up the steps to my house—through the doorway where I brought my own babies home from the hospital on their second day of life; that sanctuary now a place of fear and pain.

Inside that doorway was another woman's life, a woman who also sought sanctuary for her babies. Everything was deceptively arranged as though she had lived there for months, as the forged lease indicated. Her things, my things; the two us intertwined without my consent.

In the hours between Good Friday and Holy Saturday, we went through our-home-that-was-her-home, sorting our things from hers.

Touching with our hands the intimate mingling of ourselves and our adversary.

Never before or since have I received such a bittersweet gift, an invitation to see an enemy's life as she sees it.

Her pantry and her closets. The gifts hiding for her children's birthdays, and the homemade presents they affectionately made for her. The DVDs promising escape and a better life through romance. Postcards from televangelists promising a get-rich-quick theology. Her intimate hopes and dreams reflected in everyday things, like those we each gather around us.

In those hours of sorting, I saw how she was raised and how she lived. I saw what resources she did and did not have, her feisty courage, her brokenness, her desperate attempts and frightening failures. I saw the layers upon layers of injustice others had heaped upon her, as well as the social and systemic abuses in which we all play a part. I saw that these things were intermingled with her own wrong, illegal, and unjust choices.

But the first and overwhelming thing I saw when I looked at my perpetrator was a woman who was utterly broken, herself a victim of so much injustice and pain; and I saw that I could not pick up a stone to throw at her. Legal recourse, yes, for her sake as well as my own. But even the furious anger pulsing through me was not large enough to keep down the compassion and—yes—love I felt for her. From just a glimpse through the lens of God, who sees all things, I saw she was my sister. Yes, I had filled my life with better choices—but only after others filled me with better resources, training, encouragement, and love. That I have these things—unearned and overflowing at my disposal—does not qualify me to look down on those who do not.

To whom much is given, much will be required.

Late that night, in the middle of literal and spiritual darkness, I wrote down this cry for redemption:

She has only processed white flour and sugar, bologna and junk food—no fruits or vegetables, grain or meat. She has cable in every room but no books, games, music, or friends. She has letters and promises and formulas for wealth from God but no evidence of Good News, of Love and Grace. She has tips on how to win the lottery and a trail of short-lived employment start-date letters and pay stubs. She has love notes from her babies and school notes reporting their fights, suspensions, and failures. She has a journal of love songs and poems and court documents for her divorce and custody disputes.

She has committed crimes against us, lied to and about us, forged legal documents in our name, broken and entered our house, pushed us to the limits, and forced the loss of finances and property.

She is lost, scared, and desperate. She has nowhere to go and no one to help her. She has children and dreams of security for them and for herself. She is homeless and has a picture of a sprawling California mansion on her nightstand.

She needs mercy.

We need justice.

My longing is for restoration, but my recourse is the law.

We spend our working days advocating for the vulnerable, while advocating in our spare time for her arrest.

I am vulnerable to her crimes, and she is vulnerable to my rights.

She needs compassion but seeks help through lawlessness.

She has hurt us and is hurting.

She is the wicked and evil in my life but the broken victim in her own.

I cannot accept a redemption story that does not keep her in its deepest and most precious heart. You can see her childhood and her past, those things that molded and broke her, the life built by junk food and junk companionship.

You know it all and more.

This Easter, and in the final day, what redemption do You have in

mind? A new earth must have room for the living things that both kill us
and give us life and for this woman who is both criminal and precious
child.

I am undone.

Rebuild me according to your truth.

As the sun rose, we went home and to bed. My troubled thoughts
wandered to a friend walking through a time of darkness, meandered
next to my children, then to my husband, then to other friends and
family in their own darknesses. I pondered how each person is as
valuable to someone as my babies are to me, that somehow life is both
unfathomably precious and utterly fragile—that God-sized redemption
must swallow us all, not merely skim a little off the top.

Just after sunrise, the room floods with light, the scent of spring
flowers, and the sound of bells—the symbolism of new life, of darkness
vanquished, of Good News that interrupts all sounds of weeping. On
this Easter morning my mind is jammed with tortured thoughts, the
abstract theology of Jesus's triumph over evil juxtaposed starkly with
the crime that has overtaken my life.

She sits in jail this morning. I sit in church.

Theology, this Easter, cannot be abstract. Suffering, redemption,
grace, sin, and forgiveness stare me in the face and demand an answer.
The pain and anger in life up close means that Resurrection cannot be
limited to the safe domain of songs and stories. It cannot be contained
by those of us dressed up in the pews on Sunday.

Surrounded by jubilant celebration, I can't help but ask: What
does this mean for her? For my enemy who is my sister? And more,
what can this possibly mean for her-and-me, one entity meant
to sit and receive together the shocking news of Resurrection?

Redemption is wholeness for both of us, not one of us triumphing over the other.

When he announced his redemption of the world, to the world, he did not address only those who were only a little broken and could run to him; he did not overlook those so shattered they could neither hear his voice nor lift broken arms toward his saving hands. It is not redemption if the most broken and destroyed among us are not made whole. God's promise cannot be limited to me and those like me. If he is to make things new, then redemption includes my enemies. If God's redemptive story is true, it is true for the real world and every ugly, broken thing suffering within it. Resurrection redemption reaches all the way into death and decay.

The question pulses through me with every breath: if I understand what Easter is about, how can I celebrate it without her? The redemption initiated by Christ is not my righteousness triumphing over her lawlessness. That is simply the righteousness under the law, the former thing. But now, in Christ, a new mystery is revealed. Resurrection redemption is full restoration of her life and mine. Restoration of her life with mine.

We cannot truly celebrate alone. After all, in God's kingdom the lion will lie down with the lamb.

If I believe Christ's Easter story in its fullness and follow it to its conclusion, what can the truth be but this? And if this is true, what other truth could be large enough to overcome it?

My phone rings again.

The police officer assigned to our case asks to meet me at the condo; the woman who stole our home has agreed to leave. Even so, the law states that only she can remove her possessions from our house. Since she is in jail, her friend is coming to pack up instead.

A moving crew joins us, and as they carry clothing and furniture to the truck, they look at me quizzically. "We just moved this stuff into the condo two weeks ago. What's going on?"

My job is to be a witness, along with the police, as this friend boxes the possessions, as the movers carry them out. My heart breaks as I realize that the "friend" is a sister of a former boyfriend. The two women haven't spoken in years—yet this was the closest kin she knew to call at such a desperately dark hour.

Finally, the empty house is ours again. The sale under contract can continue toward closing. What was lost has been found. What was stolen has been redeemed.

At least, for me.

"Why on this night do we dip the herbs twice?" On Passover night, my child asks the traditional question and receives the traditional answer: The greenness of the herbs reminds us of springtime, of new life. We dip the parsley in salt to remember the weeping. We dip the bitter herbs in sweetness to recall that from suffering comes redemption.

This is deep redemption. Not pruning a bit off the top, but swallowing up from the roots. New Creation must undo and remake every broken, breaking, destructive piece and turn it to wholeness and life. Only by joining this story of redeeming power can we ever hope. Not for protection, perhaps, or safety, but for ultimate salvation and love. The sort of love that, once or twice in a lifetime, feels so tangible you could reach out and grab ahold of it.

On Resurrection Sunday, as on Passover, the bitter herbs of all our brokenness are dipped, twice. In the deepest magic of his redemption, our suffering and bondage are taken into his fathomless arms—and made green with new life.

She sits in jail; I sit at home. She chooses deception and theft against me, while I pursue her conviction. She will lose everything she sacrificed for; I will recover all I have lost. Deep redemption has not yet come, for we cannot yet sit together and rejoice, made new and set free. We are truly enemies.

And yet.

I am convinced that neither death nor life, neither angels nor demons, neither the present nor the future, nor any powers, neither height nor depth, nor anything else in all creation, will be able to separate us from the love of God that is in Christ Jesus our Lord. Even in the darkest hour. Each of us.

Entirely.

Already.

Regardless.

The matzah crumbling in my hands is broken. But it will be brought back together. Somewhere in the world-made-new my enemy and I sit and drink the wine of rejoicing, whole.

Together.

■ PRAYER

Father, teach me how to work toward new life, here in the midst of so much death. Show me a vision of a redemption that swallows us all. Amen.

■ WRITING PROMPT

How has suffering and evil led you to confront the idea of deep redemption?

Metastatic
by Katherine James

My breasts are squinting eyes now.
Worried. They slant up toward my throat
and share their sutures with the world.
They understand in ways they never did when
they laughed and hid

in linen cover.

They are recorded in backlit film,
a luminesce like the end of the world
might be if bombs hit, their sudden atoms splitting as planned
and steaming with thought like the
labeled white coat woman who
understands how crass the ordeal.

My life is death or life or death so
eyes and hands employ the malleable parts of what is left
like dough made soft by yeast.
They search.

It only takes one cell.

To travel arid roads towards what life is left,
the blood, like monster tanks, takes men, my woman,
to black desert flags stuck deep in sandy scags
like armpits up for likely mass. The IED's in wait.

My organs wait for the inevitable moment
when, hit by tombs that walk, they swallow death,
star anise not remembered. It's all new yet
old, so I think of all that have been here
where I am, machete at the neck,

and in this I cry

for them as much for me. I hold my sisters' hands and
we swing them forward, back, half smiles, because our ribs
might ache, or shins, or ropes of veins inside,
or brains. Or minds. We know eternity. Our flags are white, yet still,

my narrow eyes can't look.

■ PRAYER

Jesus, I confess to you that I am afraid of cancer, afraid of dying, afraid
of being taken from my children early. Lord, help me cast these fears
unto you and give me a newfound faith in your goodness and daily,
consistent healing work in my life. Amen.

■ WRITING PROMPT

Describe how you confronted a health crisis in yourself or in someone
close to you.

Beyond September 11th
by Nicole T. Walters

There were seeds of faith being planted in my life before I ever knew it, evidence of God's plan when I look back. Like the acorn that lies dormant on the forest floor, it seems random, accidental. But it is just lying in wait for the right time and place to become something greater.

At fourteen my life was characterized by fertile soil, ready for those seeds to take root. The only way I can explain it is that God was pursuing me long before I could put a name to the emptiness inside. Faith was new and church was foreign to me, but I wanted desperately to grow.

But for all my enthusiasm, my roots stopped shallow. It wasn't long before, grappling with how to make sense of living out a faith my family didn't share, the love was choked out by rules and the hypocrisy that surrounded me in that little youth group.

Lost in the weeds and thorns of disillusionment, I uprooted myself from it all: Church. God. Rules.

Everything about my suburban existence was challenged when I planted my life in a large public university. My self-constructed Christian bubble had already burst. Now my Deep South, middle-class, white one did, too.

I gladly launched myself into the diversity all around me while I tried to ignore the stirrings in my soul. I was unsure how to reconcile a God who was supposed to love everyone with his people who, in my experience, did not. The tiny sapling that had been my faith was not dead but found no place to grow.

By the first semester of my junior year, *I* had plans, and I didn't want to ask God for his input. In an interesting pairing of classes—

Intro to World Religions and Arabic—I simultaneously learned the basic beliefs of Islam and made my first Muslim friends.

As I grew to love my Middle Eastern friends, the tension grew inside of me. I still believed Jesus was more than the prophet my Muslim friends viewed him as, but where did they fit into his plan?

It was in this ripe place for growth that I found myself the day the world shook and the smoke rose into the sky over New York City. Many people of my generation recall September 11, 2001, as a day that changed everything—for me it was the day after.

The wounds still fresh—the normal chatter before my Arabic class was replaced with an unnatural hush. I don't know how long we sat there before our professor with kind eyes spoke quietly. Our class looked very different than most that day—the mixture of white and brown faces, the meeting of different faiths. While others that day discussed the fear of terrorism and blamed those responsible, we talked about a different kind of fear and blame.

I got to glimpse firsthand the pain of those who were at the receiving end of pointed fingers and targeted insults. Tears flowed anew as my beautiful friends spoke of their fear in being targeted because of their brightly colored headscarves, and some admitted—with much shame—that they had thought of removing them.

There were the victims of 9/11 in the official counts announced when the rubble was cleared away. But there was a whole other group of people who became victims that day. The women in hijabs. The Sikhs wearing turbans. The devout men with beards. The Muhammads and Osamas. The Khans and Alis.

In one day they were all labeled "enemy" because of their faith or their name, their language or heritage. They became feared and hated, targeted and profiled.

That night I stood amid the flickering flames of a makeshift altar. The iron arch that stood as the entrance to our North Campus was littered with flowers and candles, surrounded by weeping students.

There haven't been many times in my life I can say I heard God speak specifically or audibly to me. But in that moment the voice ringing in my ears was so clear and forceful that it brought me to my knees: "Love those who, even now, others are growing to hate. Love those who are feared and oppressed, rejected, and who have few who love them."

"I will go wherever you ask me to, Lord," I cried. "I will not let hate win in my life. I will love, and I will show your mercy and grace to anyone who needs to know it."

Jesus found me on the steps of the arch that night. And for the first time, I really found him. The soil, the light, the season—they were all just right. Everything that had led me there, all the seeds of my faith, came together in that moment as my understanding of grace began to take root.

The rebuilding began—of lives torn apart, of a Ground Zero blown to bits, and of my faith. But other destruction had begun—hatred rumbling through the world. Wars were fought, terror cells grew, an Arab Spring rose, and every day more killing occurred in the name of a misunderstood and feared faith.

That moment which launched the hatred altered the trajectory of my life, too. I fell in love with cultures not my own and began to fill my passport with Asian stamps. As I grew more deeply rooted in the all-encompassing grace of Christ, I found myself transplanted into a new land. Six years after that pivotal moment on the altar that was the university steps, I sat in another Arabic class, newly married and wide-eyed. We had moved to the Middle East to gain a deeper understanding of international life in the hopes of eventually helping start small businesses in poor and struggling communities.

When our time in the Middle East was cut short, we knew we couldn't just return and try to live the "American Dream." Back in

America, we spoke broken Arabic with the owner of a Lebanese restaurant nearby. We broke the fast during Ramadan with new friends we made at the Islamic Community Center near our hometown. We laughed together over stuffed grape leaves and strong coffee. We wanted our lives to grow into a strong and sheltering place for others. But how?

Almost fourteen years to the day since my little world exploded, I am in awe of where God has taken me. My two children sit knee to knee with their Afghan friends. The international language of art ties them together as scissors and markers are piled up between them.

We are nearby with their parents talking about what life in America looks like, filling in the gaps for the newly arrived refugees. When conversation moves to faith, we speak freely of spiritual things and offer our prayers for each other with gratitude.

We had been amazed when we discovered one of the largest refugee communities in the country is situated less than an hour from our home and that we could connect with families just arriving on our shores in pursuit of a fresh start.

Sitting there, I recall all the times I felt like an outsider—in my family, in my own faith, in living as a minority in a Muslim country. God continues to connect us with those most considered outsiders, and we also see a growing need to share what he has taught us about his love for all people as we still encounter much fear. Many churches said they would volunteer to help Christian refugees, but not Muslims. There is still a great divide to conquer.

I have seen things most would never get to witness. Visiting five developing countries in five years, I met people who had incredible stories of oppression and abuse, pain and need. I also witnessed the way the love of God can transform lives and communities.

People aren't hearing the voices of the people in those communities. They don't have a platform to tell their stories. But as an American Christian writer, I do. I heard that strong, insistent voice again in my heart—this time telling me it was my responsibility to tell of what I had seen. Their stories are my stories, too. Where my roots have grown deep into God's call to love the strangers among us, a voice to call others has emerged.

I write to tell stories of the transformation I know is possible. I know because I've lived it—once full of fear and striving, knowing nothing of grace. God taught me how to love without borders, and my life was never the same. Those seeds planted years ago have transformed into what I daily pray is a sheltering place for others to grow.

■ PRAYER

Jesus—you who pursue me with unending love and who have invited me into your family—thank you for allowing me the space to grow into a flourishing faith and for using me to communicate your grace and love to a hurting world. Show me how I can become part of the transformation you want to see in others and in welcoming the outsider. Amen.

■ WRITING PROMPT

Imagine a person whom you might extend a welcoming hand to, and describe your actions.

Blossoms

Facing the Ramp
by Trina Pockett

I 've cheated death twice in my life. The first time was at the tender age of eight.

I was a rascal. I grew up at the end of a cul-de-sac, spending most of my time playing catch until dark, learning to ride my bike without using my hands, and drawing hundreds of different hopscotch patterns on the ground. The smell of eucalyptus filled the warm evening air at our makeshift neighborhood baseball games as we took turns trying to hit a home run. The sun set behind the hills of our city, and we each were called in, one by one, for dinner. I was usually covered in sweat and dirt and, on the most unfortunate days, scrapes, scratches, and poison ivy. I didn't mind though. That's the price I paid for adventure. And I loved adventure.

I watched those boys ride by—in formation like a pack of wolves. Their bikes glistened in the sun as they passed by our mess of dolls. I wanted *so* badly to be a part of that gang. I never knew where they were headed, but the bike gang was always on the go. I was certain that they experienced epic adventures every day. I wanted to be a part of those adventures.

Being a girl lowered my chances of getting into the club. That, and the fact that my bicycle was purple with handlebar ribbons and a banana seat—complete with a basket on the front. I didn't exactly fit the BMX gang profile.

After months and months of watching them ride by, I finally got the courage to ask if I could ride along. I didn't want to lead the pack (yet); I just wanted to pedal with them for a while. To my surprise, the leader of the gang gave me permission to ride along for the day.

He probably thought that I would lose interest or that I wouldn't be able to keep up. Little did he know that this was my moment in time to prove that I was just as tough and just as brave as they were. I pedaled my little heart out and followed those boys all over the neighborhood. The faster they went, the harder I pedaled. The wind ripped through my hair and my calves burned, but I didn't care. I was free to ride with the cool bikes, explore new areas of our city, and chase adventure.

Day after day, I would run home from school, grab a snack, kiss my mom, and head out to get on my banana-seat bike. My agenda was the bike gang's agenda. Sometimes we would ride to the local market for penny candies. Other times we would make our way up to the community pool, but most of the time we just rode around the same three neighborhood blocks. We were like a family. I got the reputation as the cool younger kid, even though I was a girl. My days of pedaling had given me a certain amount of credibility with those boys.

When the bike gang got tired of pedaling, we found other activities to occupy our time. One summer day, we decided to build a dirt-bike track. Once we had our general plans for the track, we each ran home to grab whatever makeshift tools we could find. Spatulas, buckets, bowls, and other random kitchen items were added to our tool pile. Using these tools, we began to dig, sculpt, and shape our track. Mostly, I was the errand girl, retrieving shovels, picking up nails, and running home to get snacks for the workers. After what seemed a lifetime of work, we completed the track.

Everyone enjoyed their inaugural ride around the track, going over little mounds of dirt, turning on a dime, careening to a stop, impressing the crowd. Oddly enough, each biker avoided the colossal jump in the middle of the track. It was the elephant in the room—everyone knew it was there, but no one wanted to attempt it. If the jump was not executed correctly, it was certain death.

Where those boys saw fear, I saw an opportunity. Making that jump just might prove my abilities to the bike gang. I spoke before I had time to think about it. "I'll take the jump!" I shouted. Every head turned my way in disbelief. I, too, was shocked that I said it. I slowly walked forward, allowing my bike to lead my reluctant feet. Panic started to sweep over me as I made my way to the front of the pack. The oldest boy asked me if I really wanted to attempt the jump. I think he was trying to give me an out. My pride (and youthful stupidity) kept me from running the other way. I gave an uncertain nod, and in that moment my gang status jumped from low girl on the totem pole to cool kid. I was in my glory, basking in the accolades. Yes, I, Trina Whipple, would be the first to attempt the jump.

I faced the ramp, and with all the courage that I could muster, I put one foot on the pedal and pushed down. With the momentum of the hill, I picked up speed quickly. Thoughts raced through my mind. Would I crash? Could I take a quick left and ride home? What if I actually landed this? I would be launched into neighborhood stardom. As the ramp got closer, I started to panic. What did the boys say? Lean into it? Lift the bike? I couldn't remember. My bike started to ascend on the ramp. My vision blurred, and I could feel my heartbeat in my teeth. My front wheel started to roll over the edge. My hands gripped tight around my handlebars. Just as soon as my bike got close to the edge, I made a critical error: I leaned forward. It doesn't take a rocket scientist to figure out that when you lean forward, your body and bike follow suit. I barely made if off of the ramp before my bike slammed into the ground below. It wasn't even a graceful fall. Legs and wheels were flopping every which way. A burst of dirt clouded around me. I had officially crashed and, in my mind, failed.

I opened my eyes to see if I was dead. Nope, still alive. The shock of the crushing pain settled in. I slowly untangled myself from the bike. The boys ran over to help me up; one even showed some tenderness by asking if I was okay. The best case was a perfect landing. The worst case was death. I was somewhere right in the middle between best and worst. I walked home—with blood running down my knees and a bruised ego.

As I write about that life experience now, I think of it from a completely different perspective. Not as a little girl who took the jump and failed miserably, but as a little girl who had the bravery to take the jump. Sometimes growth is painful. Little did I know I would need that type of bravery later in life—the type of bravery that requires fearless pedaling toward the unknown. Pedaling toward what could be a perfect jump or a miserable crash landing.

I needed that same brave heart on a day, many years later, when I was sitting in the hospital. The moment is seared into my memory. Three words tore through the pages of my history. My memories would always be divided into chapters of before and after that day.

I was a twenty-three-year-old mom lying on a doctor's exam table waiting to see my baby on the monitor. After a few minutes of searching, a magical pixelated image of our daughter showed up on the screen. The image was accompanied by the sound of the heartbeat. The steady rhythm was more beautiful than any symphony.

The technician took her time taking measurements and assuring me that my baby looked healthy. Her frequent kicking and moving confirmed what I already knew—she was growing strong.

The technician offered me a paper towel to wipe the jelly off of my belly. She helped me sit up; in those days, I needed help with the simplest tasks. Tying my shoes proved to be the biggest feat. The doctor entered the room to congratulate me and ask if I had any follow-up questions. I was quickly reminded of an annoying walnut-sized lump on the side of my neck. The lump didn't cause much pain, so I had dismissed it. I mentioned it to the doctor, and no sooner had I said the words than her face changed from comfort to concern. She reached up and felt the lump with two fingers. She slowly moved away, picking my chart up off the counter.

Idle chat stopped, and the air in the room changed. Though I felt the awkward shift, I was still in elation at the news of being pregnant with a girl. The doctor jotted a few notes and then told me that she'd really like for me to meet with the ear, nose, and throat specialist. I told her that I would make an appointment first thing, to which she responded, "I mean right now." I was surprised by her concern and honestly a little annoyed.

I did what I was told and went to the office across the hall. Clearly, they knew that I was coming because I was immediately escorted into an exam room. A tall, athletic young doctor entered the room a few minutes later. He asked a few questions and then proceeded to feel the lump on the base of my neck. Same reaction: quiet withdrawal, then notes on the chart.

He said that he was uncomfortable with the lump and that he'd like to do an emergency biopsy. Those are two words that a pregnant woman does not want to hear: *emergency* and *biopsy*. The doctor was emphatic that a biopsy was incredibly important. This test would help rule out any serious conditions. I thanked him for his time, and as I made my way up to the scheduling desk, I stopped in the hallway to make sense of what had happened. How did I go from elation to confusion in such short time? I felt like I had just heard a tornado siren, and the wind was picking up momentum. (Little did I know, I would be like Dorothy in the scene from *The Wizard of Oz* when she is trying to outrun the storm. In the toughest moments, I was certain the storm would win.)

Two days later, I checked into the hospital for a routine biopsy. They administered medicine into my IV, and I fell asleep. When I woke up I was foggy, disconnected. It took me a minute to remember where I was. The doctor opened the door and walked over to my bed. He reached down to hold my hand, and with the most sincere eyes he said the three words that changed everything: "You have cancer."

I'm not the only woman in the world who has faced daunting circumstances. As women, we are no strangers to adversity. It rears its ugly head in many ways: loss of a job, depression, relationship issues, illness, miscarriage, infertility, addiction, divorce, and so on. Women have struggled, fought, and trudged through hurts of all kinds.

I have traveled uncertain roads, just as you have, roads that lead to detours—finding a lump; hearing that your husband is leaving you; meeting with your boss when he tells you that he has to let you go because of budget cuts; being told by the police officer at your door that your child has been in a car accident. We all face unexpected moments and uncertainty in life.

Every woman has her own version of these moments. Some of you are walking a hard road right now. The question isn't *if* we will experience the pain and heartache of life, but *when* we will experience it. And more importantly, how we will change because of it.

I faced the cancer storm, but I didn't do it alone. I had a family who loved me, a team of doctors who meticulously calculated the correct dosage of chemotherapy to administer. I was surrounded by a group of incredible women who held me up when I couldn't stand alone—they watched my son, brought us food, prayed for me, sat with me during the endless hours of chemotherapy. And on that incredible July morning that I delivered Kate into this world, they celebrated with me.

The key is that, whatever comes our way, we must stand committed to grow *in community*. I grew up in the middle of redwood country. Some of the local redwood trees are taller than 350 feet. They are majestic trees. The secret about the redwood trees is that, though they are tall, they have very shallow roots. Their roots intertwine with each other underground so that they won't fall. They stand up together! It's the perfect picture of a growing, supportive community.

Adversity in life *will* challenge us, stretch us, and reshape us, causing tremendous growing pains, but there is hope to be found in the process. We learn more about ourselves, our faith, and our ability to overcome.

Finding that lump forced me to find that brave little girl inside. The girl who was willing to face the ramp, pedal her heart out, and take the jump. In the moments of uncertainty, we all need to find that courage—that childlike faith that we will make it. It might hurt, but we will make it. And in the end, we will be stronger women because of what we have faced.

Who knows how we will land in this crazy life? What matters is that we keep pedaling. So find that brave little girl inside of you, hop on your bike, and take the jump. The world is waiting for you.

■ PRAYER

Heavenly Father, I thank you for your love and your grace in my life. Sometimes life can be so hard. Please show me how I can share your love with people who are hurting. Help me to trust you in all situations—even the most painful. Help me to be brave when I feel weak. Help me to find peace in the uncertainty of the world. And above all, help me to find rest in you. I ask this in your Son's perfect holy name. Amen.

■ WRITING PROMPT

Think about a time when you were brave. How did you experience community in this moment? How can you create a space of community for people who are hurting?

My First Padded Bra
by Leslie Leyland Fields

The year I was to turn fifty I had plans. Big plans. I was going to get my first manicure. I was going to run my first marathon. I was going to climb Mt. Kilimanjaro with Joni on her fiftieth birthday. Then, my hips and joints started getting cranky. My budget for international travel seized up. I forgot about the manicure. Instead, I had a party with fifty friends. And after that, I did it. I bought my first padded bra.

I'm not exactly sure how it happened. It wasn't premeditated. I was traveling and ended up in a department store, slinking undercover through the lingerie section. (Never quite sure I belong there.) Then— brain flash—I could repay my husband for Mr. Momming the week I was away with a sexy little something. Usually it was the foreign import section for me, but the padded bras beckoned—objects of both fascination and repulsion. I had never worn one. They looked like foamy dishes and came in an astounding range, from little tea cups to Italian restaurant-size bowls. And the sizing is the same as batteries. But no size was my size. (Even batteries come in AAA!) Then on a little end rack, I found it. A flirty, spongy little number that looked small enough to fit.

I've worn sports bras most of my life. Not the fitted ones—the stretchy fill-as-you-can kind. I've felt their power all these years. No matter what I was wearing on the outside, underneath I felt sporty, ready to break into a jog or an aerobic routine at any moment. And often I did. My bra inspired me. I've always taken pleasure in my boyishness and the freedom it brought. I've felt like Peter Pan refusing to grow up, my chest proof I was still young, nubile, and mobile.

Despite our culture's unflagging obsession with breasts, I've never felt insecure about mine. They may be less decorative than others, but few have enjoyed the same utility. Mine have fed people—six, actually—grew them from mewling newborn to stalwart near-toddler. A full six years logged on these breasts, boosting closeness, intelligence, and immunities for us both, a whole string of benefits conferred from my milk-rich low-fat deposits.

But my freshman year of high school I would have traded with anyone. Breasts were so much in demand that year that tissue-stuffed bras became something of a norm, a trend I joined while hoping for nature to take its usual hormonal course. I soon gave up on the venture, especially after my tissues crept unbidden out of my shirt one day in plain view of the boy I had a crush on. When I saw his eye wander downward, I should have simply yanked out a tissue with a flourish and blown my suddenly stuffy nose, winking seductively like, *Aren't we girls inventive creatures who can stow the most necessary items in such mystical places?*

I do recall a few other moments, in college, when I layered a second bra over my first, aiming for some kind of collegial shape to my body. To at least belong among the freshman femininity parading before the male upperclassmen, whom we knew were surveying the goods as we clicked by on our heels, swishing our skirts. (Yes, we wore high heels and [modest] skirts. This was a Christian college where "the men looked like men and the women looked like women." A great obsession of conservative Christians in the unisex hippie days of flowing hair, platform shoes, and jeans.)

But this new bra—all foamy and thick, plush in just the right places—was more. This was not a tame bra; it was leopard-spotted.

I wear it now nearly every day. I wear it so no one will notice me. If anyone thought to comment on my new look, they might say, "There's a middle-aged woman in a polka-dot blouse," instead of, "There's a middle-aged woman without any breasts." I look better in my clothes,

I discovered—after all these years. My blouses don't bag in the front. My waist looks slightly smaller (a new curiosity since menopause is setting in). I like it. For the first time since my nursing days, I am thinking that breasts are a good idea. Maybe God knew something here. I'm happy to be able to strap some on when I want them. And I'm sometimes relieved to take them off.

I think I'm beginning to understand why women want breasts. Most women have them anyway, and since it's one of the major ways we're distinguished from men, why not celebrate and even exaggerate the distinction? Why not dress to highlight the obvious? (But then, that next step, why not have my body cut open to insert little baggies of salt water or silicone . . . ?)

I'm not a total dunce. I know it's about power and sex—all that. I remember that kind of power. In my twenties and thirties, when I traveled alone, men would try to flirt with me (me, in my rubber-band bra), angling for a number, whatever they could extract. I never played. They were so pathetically obvious, and I was obviously ring-on-the-finger married, uninterested. Still, looking back, it was flattering.

Maybe I'm fooling myself now, and really I just want some of that power back. Aging is about as much fun as I anticipated twenty or so years ago. And I'm not sure women are getting much help. Women's magazines could do better. I'm a sucker for inspirational articles: makeup makeovers, wardrobe do-overs, hair fix-its, fat-to-thin befores and afters. But on the "older woman" front, I'm continually disappointed. Invariably the magazines feature women in their forties, fifties, and sixties who are still knockouts. "Look! You may be older, but you can still be gorgeous!" is the message. But these chosen ones, who look better at sixty than most of us looked at twenty, were, first of all, born gorgeous, and second, much of their current looks come via airbrushing, implants, surgeries, liposuction, lasers, and tucks, to name just a few interventions. Is this the best we can do? This summarily dumps us all back in ninth grade. Are we still coining our value on our looks? Have we learned nothing in the decades since?

Movies aren't much better. In a movie I watched recently, a twenty-eight-year-old guy falls for Michelle Pfeiffer, who's twenty years older. Of course he falls for her. She's the craziest-beautiful fifty-year-old woman I've ever seen (and the craziest-beautiful forty-year-old, thirty-year-old—you get the drift). Of course he doesn't notice her age—she doesn't look her age! (What if she did? What if she were thirty pounds heavier—the size of a normal fifty-year-old, that is? What if she didn't have those lips, those hips?) The whole setup is patently unfair and does not—I repeat to well-meaning moviemakers, *does not*—inspire older women to believe in themselves.

And I hope I never see another article on Tina Turner, who is famous for her unending incredibly toned legs, usually festooned in fishnets and exposed nearly all the way up. And she is nearing seventy. Yes, it's incredible. Yes, Tina Turner, you have fabulous legs, better than any *fifty*-year-old I know. Congratulations, you lucky woman, you. Now what? We put the magazine down and avoid the mirror. We end up believing the same old message from high school: If you've still got it, you're a player. If not, game over.

Last month, I spent some time with a friend from college. We're the same age. She's had breast implants, Botox, an eye lift, full facial laser treatment, a fat transfer, and I don't know what else. She's also much thinner than me and dresses like a *Vogue* cover girl. She looks fantastic. When I'm with her, I'm invisible. Everyone rubbernecks—men, women, children. I watch them watch her—relieved actually.

I love her a lot, but I don't want to be her, I recently realized. I don't want to be that noticed. I've come to some other realizations lately, inspired by the new decade I'm wearing. I'm trying to feel good about myself and my increasingly visible changes, but feeling good isn't enough. I read an article in a semireligious digest last month that instructed women to start their day by standing in front of the mirror, wrapping their arms around themselves, and reciting, "I love you! You're so beautiful!" as many times as they needed, an unabashed hail-to-the-self.

Surely there's more to feeling good about ourselves than feeling good about ourselves. I think there is. I see it on the faces of a few women I know in their seventies and eighties, women with wide waists, sagging chests, and creased, smiling faces, faces brightly turned to others. These are women who feel good about themselves, but clearly they feel even better about others.

Truth be told, I envy Michelle Pfeiffer and the other menopausal women who look so great, but I'm saving my admiration for the women who truly are great. Who are so busy being themselves and doing good work at home and out in the world that they don't have the time or the interest to worry about their wrinkles or their bustline. I see some of these women at my local coffee shop, at church, at my father's nursing home, in the hospital waiting room. Women who love others completely, with abandon. No one's taking their picture. They're almost invisible—at first.

I'm not one of them. My vanity still props me against the mirror every morning massaging high-promise creams into the latest creases and lines. I'm always trying to lose ten pounds. I wear shocking red lipstick, splurge occasionally on a froufrou coat, fret about my varicose veins. At fifty-seven now, I still want to look and feel good. But more than that—and more than ever—I want to be good. I want to be the kind of person who sees beyond herself to others around her. The kind who loves her neighbor like herself, who does for others what she would like others to do for her, two golden rules that never show their age. When I see others doing this, it's so beautiful that it takes my breath away.

I'm trying to practice this now, some days in my padded bra. But I may not wear it forever. Ten or twenty years from now, maybe I'll be back to my sports bra. If anyone should notice me, in a coffee shop, church, or a hospital, leaning toward others in laughter, in friendship, in service, maybe they'll say, "Look at that happy old woman in that red lipstick and polka-dotted blouse."

Or maybe, older and wiser, they'll simply say, "Look at that beautiful woman."

■ PRAYER

Jesus, thank you for fearfully and wonderfully making me a woman. Please continue to comfort me and give me a Holy Spirit–inspired appreciation for my body as I age. May I have your eyes for the heart and not obsess on the external. Thank you, Lord. Amen.

■ WRITING PROMPT

What does it mean to you to "everbloom"—to remain beautiful, thriving, confident, and blossoming at any age?

Metamorphosis of Me
by Ilona K. Hadinger

I saw the soul whose name is Me,
Viewing only imperfection;
The shyness, the insecurity,
the calloused introspection.
No courage of heart,
blind to inner endowments,
Shackled
By perpetual disguisements
           Of smiles and laughter.

I saw the face whose name is Me,
relying on its comeliness;
The dark eyes, the complexion,
the countenance luminous.
No conspicuous flaws,
delighting in my configuration,
Bound
With want of inner formation
           Of depth and purpose.

God saw the soul whose name is Me,
abounding in capacity;
The kindness, the meekness,
the love with voracity.
No judgments false,
alive to deep ambition

Committed
To see my fruition
          Of growth and calling.

God saw His creation whose name is Me,
warning of all vanity;
The charms, the beauty,
fading long before eternity.
No hope in deceit,
casting truthful illumination,
Compelled
To reveal my destination
          Of work and mission.

I engaged the words whose author is God,
reading with veneration;
Fearfully? Wonderfully?
Is it true this exclamation?
Not perfect in spirit,
yet with resolute insurgence
Determined
To experience an emergence
          Of grace and belief.

I gripped the words whose author is God,
responding in gratitude;
My will, my heart,
all His in plenitude!
Not empty religion,
but a holy invitation,
Amazed
By the Son's vindication
          Of sin and conceit.

God engaged the soul whose name is Me,
Infusing such vitality;
My bones, my being,
reviving with conformity.
Not coercion or duty,
rather joyful exuberance,
Intent
To offer preponderance
          Of life and eternity.

God gripped the soul whose name is Me,
Whispering a declaration:
Your life, your purpose,
fulfilled in peregrination.
Not earthly roots,
But a heavenly residence,
Absolute
For future providence
          Of home and glory.

I see this soul whose name is Me,
Overcoming imperfection,
The shyness, the insecurity,
Replaced in resurrection!
New courage of heart,
Aware of inner endowments,
Freed
By sincere respondence
          Of yea and amen.

God sees this soul whose name is Me
Abounding in great capacity

With kindness, with meekness,
To love with voracity.
New justice true,
born in deep ambition
Committed
To bring fruition
Of growth and calling.

■ PRAYER

Heavenly Father, I know you see me and love me as I am, yet I thank you for your greater love not to leave me as I am. I surrender to you in transformation. I place my life in your hands, embracing your purpose and calling in my life. Lead me and guide me as I bravely pursue and develop the gifts and desires you've given me. I look forward to the fruition of my growth and calling, for the sake of your kingdom! In Jesus's name. Amen.

■ WRITING PROMPT

Describe a season of metamorphosis in your life.

When a Baby Dies
by PeggySue Wells

love to say her name, feeling the word on my tongue and hearing the sound. "Violet."

Awaiting Kicks

Moving into the fifth month of pregnancy, I was awaiting the butterfly kicks I should feel any day. But the movements didn't come. The doctor searched for a heartbeat until the batteries in the Doptone fetal monitor were drained and the silence confirmed my fears.

Our baby had died.

The sad news caught my children completely by surprise. Feeling as though we were drowning in grief, we gathered in the family room and cried. The children named the baby Trust because we were learning to trust God when we didn't understand.

An Early Birth

Another woman who lost a baby at sixteen weeks asked about my plans for the baby's arrival. That was when our family stopped waiting for a miscarriage and began preparation for an early birth.

My eight-year-old son wanted to build a casket as his gift to our baby. He spent a Saturday afternoon crafting a piece of California redwood into a small casket barely larger than a bread pan. To line the miniature box, Leilani, fourteen, stitched a doll-sized blanket from a piece of my wedding dress. Five-year-old Estee cut yellow-and-white-checked cotton to swaddle the baby. Holly, eleven, collected dried petals from the many floral arrangements friends had sent. AmyRose, sixteen, helped me gather birth supplies.

Grieving Differently

Each family member dealt with his or her grief differently. My husband was emotionally distant. Leilani and Estee cried often. Holly was angry with God. AmyRose and I found comfort in a to-do list, doing what each day required. Josiah had been praying daily for this baby, planning to share his favorite things, including locations of the bird nests, the best fishing spots, and his tree fort in the woods. He was at loose ends. I explained that having taken an early journey home, this tiny child now was waiting for Josiah's future arrival in eternity, with plans to show him the wonders there, and how vital it was that he keep the faith.

Information about how long it takes to miscarry naturally when a baby dies in utero is sketchy, but it is usually between six weeks and three months. Three-and-a-half months after the baby died, I was still pregnant. After several opinions, my doctor and I opted for the mildest form of intervention to induce labor. I wanted to birth my baby.

After I carried her seven months, on April 30, Violet Trust was born peacefully and miraculously at home. For each of us, receiving her into our family was an unparalleled wonder akin to opening our most precious Christmas gift. We hadn't known she was a girl until we held her. The size of my hand, her body was perfect and lovely.

The only part missing was life.

Each of my daughters has a flower in her name, and Violet was the unanimous choice, especially appropriate because in her perfect petiteness she resembled the spring violets in full bloom when she was born.

Early Journey Home

We buried Violet Trust on May 1. We took pictures of our tiny daughter; my favorite is the photo of her next to my wedding ring. We tenderly swaddled her in the cloth Estee prepared and wrapped her in Leilani's white satin blanket. After we placed her in the casket Josiah had made, the box was only half-full. Estee and three-year-old Hannah brought out a basket of gifts they had made for the coming baby. Lovingly created yarn dolls, bead necklaces, and carefully colored pictures filled the wooden box to the brim. Holly added dried flower petals. Violet was nestled in a box filled with gifts of love from her family and friends.

Nothing was left to do but nail the top on the casket. The ringing of the hammer sounded devastatingly final. We read aloud poems and Scripture that friends had sent to encourage our hearts. We prayed and sang worship songs.

Everything within me protested as we laid Violet in her final resting place. I didn't want my baby to be cold, wet, or alone.

On a homemade cross, painted white, the children wrote Violet Trust Wells. Over her grave we planted a Rose of Sharon and a multitude of purple-and-white wood violets. Each of us stops by that special spot often and wonders . . .

Friends did not know what to say to ease our pain. There was nothing to say. Yet we were comforted that they cared.

We are thankful for the time we had with Violet. Heaven is more precious because we have an investment there. On Violet's one-year birthday, I walked to her grave with her brand new baby sister in my arms. I told Lilyanna Faith that she has an older sister named Violet Trust.

Violet's birth announcement had these words:

We didn't get to run with you, but you beat us to heaven.
We didn't get to teach you, but you taught us to trust.
We didn't get to hear you, but you taught us to listen.

We didn't get to bathe you, but you washed us with tears.
We didn't get to comb your hair, but your beauty is beyond
*   expectation.*
We didn't get to change your diaper, but you forever changed our
*   hearts.*
We didn't get to sit on our porch together, but we see your place
*   of rest.*
We didn't get to ride the horse with you, but you are now with the
*   Creator of all.*
We didn't get to play music with you, but today you hear the
*   heavenly choir.*
We didn't get to raise you, but you raised our heads towards Him
*   whom we can trust.*
We love you, Violet Trust.

When someone loses a loved one, what do I say? How can I be the hands of Jesus to someone suffering loss?

I have found that in times of deep grief, hope is more important than advice. Job said it this way:

Is my strength the strength of stones,
Or is my flesh bronze?
Is it that my help is not within me,
And that deliverance is driven from me?
For the despairing man there should be kindness from his friend;
So that he does not forsake the fear of the Almighty. (Job 6:12–14
NASB)

During the dark hours, Jesus calls us not to be experts but to come alongside and provide encouragement.

"A friend sent flowers on that first sad Mother's Day after my mom died," my Sunday school teacher said. "I felt loved and understood."

Thankfully I don't have to have my life all together to help someone else. My sister's children died in an auto accident. "Some people felt awkward when they saw me and turned away," she shared. "I appreciated those who hugged me and said, 'I'm praying for you.'"

Trusting God when we least understand is faith in action. Gentle comfort comes from those who put their arms around hurting people and say, "I don't understand either. But I love you, and I am here to go through this with you." Paul promises, "For I am convinced that neither death nor life, neither angels nor demons, neither the present nor the future, nor any powers, neither height nor depth, nor anything else in all creation, will be able to separate us from the love of God that is in Christ Jesus our Lord" (Rom. 8:38–39 NIV).

After a long illness, a coworker's husband died. She recalled, "I was comforted by those who walked with me in the church parking lot, who sat with me so I wouldn't be alone in my regular pew, and who invited me to lunch on an otherwise lonely weekend afternoon."

We can walk beside another through the journey of grief. "If either of them falls down, one can help the other up. But pity anyone who falls and has no one to help them up" (Eccles. 4:10 NIV).

The first year after the loss of someone special is especially difficult. Holidays mercilessly remind us that life is forever altered. On Valentine's Day, Easter, Mother's or Father's Day, birthdays, wedding anniversaries, Thanksgiving, Christmas, and New Year's—I can comfort a grieving friend with flowers, a note, or a memorial gift in their loved one's name. I can soothe the sorrow of the anniversary date that marks the loss with a phone call to say, "I'm remembering you today."

The best consolation often comes from one who has been there. Our sufferings are not wasted in God's economy—"the Father of compassion and the God of all comfort, who comforts us in all our troubles, so that we can comfort those in any trouble with the comfort we ourselves receive from God" (2 Cor. 1:3b–4 NIV).

Saying Good-Bye

My grandma placed a memorial rose at the front of the church the week after she buried her husband. Following the church service, a woman widowed the year before asked Grandma what she would do now.

"Go home, I guess," Grandma answered.

"Let's get a beer," the widow teased.

The absurd idea made Grandma laugh for the first time in months. Actually, the two women went out for a milkshake—because that widow remembered how unfair life felt going home alone the first Sunday after her own husband had died.

After his wife passed away, my neighbor felt completely lost. His wife had always done the shopping, and now just seeing the variety in the detergent aisle was daunting. Widowed several years earlier, his friend remembered how terrified he had been navigating his way around the grocery aisles without his own wife. He offered to take my neighbor on his first trip to the market.

Called to mirror Jesus Christ by being his hands to a hurting world, I help others by seeing and empathizing with their pain. God consoles us so we can be God's hands of compassion to others.

I would never have wanted my friend to say good-bye to her baby at sixteen-weeks gestation. But from her experience, she was able to say the words that changed how my family approached our loss—from preparing for a funeral to preparing for a birth. Because of the empathy of a friend, I saw my opportunity to love abundantly even when it came with heartbreak. Because Violet took an early journey home, we barely said hello before saying good-bye. I'm thankful we said hello.

■ PRAYER

Thank you, God, because even though you knew I would disappoint and break your heart, you chose to love me unconditionally. Thank you for authoring this abundant life and being my constant. According to Ephesians 3:16–19, strengthen me with power through your Spirit in my inner being, so that Christ may dwell in my heart through faith— that I, being rooted and grounded in love, may be able to comprehend with all the saints what is the breadth and length and height and depth, and to know the love of Christ that surpasses knowledge, that I may be filled with all the fullness of God. In Christ's name I pray. Amen.

■ WRITING PROMPT

Every relationship at some point will bring heartbreak. Write a fictional piece about how you imagine living a life full blast, full out, and full of love, even when there are moments of disappointment.

Bittersweet
by Suzanne Burden

write the word *bittersweet* on a white napkin, pushing it across the table toward our exchange student. His eyes absorb the word as he rolls it around on his tongue, his French accent punctuating it, his mind reaching to digest it. In French, they call it *un moment doux-amer*: a bittersweet moment.

I relive the feelings with him as we talk over lunch, the high emotions he felt as he walked out of his U.S. high school for the last time. The friends and teachers he would miss. The way he fell in love with the school after all, even though it was bigger and crazier than his small French village. The reality that he will not see some of these friends again.

"Bittersweet," he says more firmly now, glad to name the feeling.

It is a mother's job to help a child name things. With English fluency as the goal, I regularly named things for him. At the beginning of his student exchange year, I would point and say, "This is my nose; these are my eyes; this is my mouth." Learning a new language and a foreign culture at the same time, this talkative yet reserved French teenager showed me the wonder of a three-year-old, the curiosity of a twelve-year-old, and the drama of a sixteen-year-old up all wrapped up in one.

The first week, Isak routinely panicked unless he knew where I was—whether he was at Walmart, at the swimming pool, or even when waiting for us to come home. As he explored his new world, he needed me as a mother, a guide, and a friend.

Isak and I shared a right-brained, intuitive, creative view of the world. There was now a human being within my home who noticed my new haircut, made dramatic statements about dreadfully ordinary occurrences, and plumbed the depths of human existence in daily conversations. I was smitten with mother-love.

Yet the story with our host son was born from *amère douleur* or bitter sorrow. Our guest room, destined to be a nursery, lay empty.

"Not everyone who wants a child gets a child," I tried to explain to others who thought late marriage, infertility, and three failed adoptions just meant we needed to keep working at it to become parents.

The baby was due on August 13. Instead, sixteen-year-old Isak arrived with jet lag and exhaustion on August 16. "This is like Wisteria Lane," he said, as we drove into our neighborhood, and we laughed, rueful grins on our faces.

I sit next to my husband on our navy-blue loveseat, a blank expression on my face.

The birth mother sits across from us on a sweetheart red upholstered chair. She is hardly able to get the words out of her mouth. My husband mutters some words like, "Well, thank you for telling us now."

I recall it even now as the day hope died.

Two months earlier, she had sat at our dining-room table over a piping-hot bowl of homemade beef stew. She had told us she had chosen us to be her baby's parents. She had promised this adoption would not be like the others.

And she had said: "And I will never change my mind."

She was an acquaintance with whom I had shared our desire to adopt. She said she never wanted to parent at all and wanted to finish her college degree, to travel, to experience the world. She had placed a baby for adoption years ago. For two months, she insisted that she wanted her baby with us, and we relented. But the questions haunted us: Do we still want this? At ages forty-two and forty-nine? Can this be trusted?

Now our birth mother sits across from me, her whole body rigid as her mouth moves. But what about the first ultrasound? And the pregnancy clothes we found for her? The meetings and the messages? What about when she called us the day she fell down the stairs? Mercifully she and baby were not hurt.

And what about the day she phoned to let me know the baby was a girl—and I screamed or squealed, I can never remember which? I remember how we were partners, she and I, in this unfolding drama. How she gave us her own childhood baby blanket for the baby. How natural it was to encourage her; how excited I was about her graduation that December; how I pictured us being there with baby in tow.

She says unfolding family dynamics caused her to question her decision. She wants to become a parent after all. I had felt her uneasiness for the past week. I knew something was off, but my husband and I had promised up front: we would never pressure her or coerce her. If this was to happen, it would happen on her initiative.

I somehow manage to speak then, interrupting my thoughts: "But . . . you did all this. You pursued us."

"Yes. And I wish I hadn't."

My whole body continues to register shock. "We are heartbroken," I say. "Not only because of the baby but because we have come to care for you. Because we care for you now, and it will no longer work for us to have a relationship. That will be taken from us, too."

When she rises, I hug her. She is stiff as a board.

I tell her once again, "We still believe you can do anything." As she walks to the front door, tears leak out of her eyes. I close the door behind her.

The day hope died I went to bed and pounded my fists on the mattress, screaming at God, "How dare you do this to us? We didn't even ask for the adoption! We felt we could never weather such a loss again. We've done nothing to deserve this!"

"Ditto!" my husband moaned from the other side of the bed.

This was no time for carefully reasoned theology, for neat boxes and tidy categories. We were keyed up for lament and anger, for raw pain and shaking fists.

For months, I felt like Naomi in the Old Testament book of Ruth, who wept bitterly, and with good reason. I purposed to ignore those who minimized our pain. I journaled, and fed my soul with theological truth about God's love for me even when I couldn't feel it. I cried while praying, and I decided to do so until the clouds started to rise.

July 31, just thirteen days from the baby's due date, I realized I missed our birth mother. I wondered how she was doing and whether she was getting the support she needed. Yet I noticed that the heaviness was starting to lift. All of the sitting still with Jesus, the lament, the tears, the realization of his love, the quietness where no words were spoken, was accomplishing something internally. Somehow, though perhaps I could not see how, all would be well.

An e-mail pinged on my phone, and I looked down. With the school year just two weeks away, the local high school had one more slot for an exchange student to fill. Addressed to a group, it was a last-minute call: Was anyone interested in hosting an exchange student?

I paused. Something in me that day wanted to reject the script I had been handed. I couldn't articulate it at the time, but I desperately wanted to be a coworker with God in my story. I was tired of being defeated by our lack. Perhaps the year would not end with only more sadness and sorrow; perhaps there was something we might do about it.

I felt, then, that the Holy Spirit was prompting me to ask my husband a simple question: "Would bringing an exchange student into our home this year bring you joy?" He had just sauntered in from work, and time seemed frozen, suspended. I expected a "maybe next year." But ten to fifteen seconds of silence ended with: "Yes."

Within forty-eight hours, we had been approved as host parents. How strange it was to watch a bedroom meant for a nursery quickly transformed into a bedroom for a sixteen-year-old. Sarah, the coordinator, had her eye on a teen named Isak from a small village in France. His student-exchange profile was filled with superlatives and exclamation points. He was excited to come to the United States to see the skyscrapers and so many other things; we were growing excited to welcome him.

When a couple is pursuing adoption, they make a profile of their own for prospective birth parents, filled with pictures and information about themselves. The front of ours contained a picture of us laughing together on the sofa with the caption: "Our home is filled with love and laughter, quiet trust and open arms." Did we still have that to give? Or had some of it evaporated under the weariness of our accumulated losses?

We painted the closet doors in Isak's bedroom, nabbed a used pine desk for his studies, and refinished a dresser. Truth be told, all was set in place hours before he arrived.

There was no way to avoid our bittersweet moment of releasing to lay hold of something different and new. We had only to trust enough to take the next step and enter into it.

As Isak exited the plane, seeing me holding the "Welcome Isak" sign with eagerness, he looked a bit startled and exhausted all at once. He gave me half of a French air kiss in greeting, as I was not practiced in receiving it. Later, he would exclaim: "I just kept thinking, these are the people with whom I will spend ten months of my life!"

Already three days late for school, Isak was overwhelmed by the high school. He hardly understood what the teachers said, as it flew by so fast. He once said, "I am shocked by everything all the time;

now I just expect that being shocked all the time is normal." It was the boisterous ways students pushed each other in the school halls between classes; it was twenty-minute lunch breaks instead of two-hour ones; it was the sloppy and "non-French" way of dressing.

We worked with teachers to try to get him help, and he worked harder than he probably ever had. He was scrappy and determined, but this was so hard. Amid the struggles, we somehow found time to delve deep into the mysteries of life as he reasoned his way through complex issues until, often, I would insist we talk about something more lighthearted, that we come up for air.

The first time I remember him truly smiling was over a pan of unbaked chocolate cookies. The act of baking cookies was a cross-cultural place of joy and contentment for him—a connector between his French world four thousand miles away and his U.S. world in which all was foreign.

One weekend, Isak asked something about children. Although I don't remember how it was phrased, our story came tumbling out through tears: The birth mother. Her asking us to adopt her baby. Us supporting her. Her changing her mind. Him coming just three days after the baby was due.

His sensitive face filled with grief, and I wished instantly that I could soften the blow. I didn't want this to be too much for him, and yet it was his question that had brought the story to the surface. I didn't want to pretend; I respected his wanting to know and understand why we did not have our own children.

"This is an injustice," I remember him saying sadly. "Why are some people never having children who want them? And then others getting pregnant who don't want their babies?"

I nodded. I had to agree with him that there are some things in life that don't appear to make sense. But there is still love through it all. For me that love originates in God, who neither wills our childlessness nor looks down on us for it, but weeps with us in the brokenness and pain.

Through the moments and days that autumn, Isak's struggle to learn English, to study, and to fit in was a bittersweet gift in itself. David and I were given the opportunity to transfer our attention from ourselves to Isak. We found tutors, we took impromptu walks, we played games, and we initiated spontaneous adventures. Every day brought discovery and healing to our hearts. We were finding new ways to appreciate each other.

With the holidays, Isak's childlike wonder burned brightly, and David and I received hand-painted frames filled with photos of us together: *Merry Christmas to my favorite host mother!* and *Merry Christmas to my favorite host father!* After the holiday break, we practically had a new teenager in our home. He was comfortable, less homesick, and excited about the things that had once shocked him.

Driving home from our spring-break trip, Isak's music was blaring through the car—a mix of French and English tunes—when we were surprised by Whitney Houston's "I Will Always Love You."

"Isak," I said quietly, "you know we will always love you, no matter what?"

"Yes," he said from the back seat, "I know that."

I began to fear how fond we were becoming of Isak, how our temporary family was melding together. Family and friends were crazy about him as well.

Oh, how will you let him go? I had no idea.

Of all the days of the year, Mother's Day for me is consistently the hardest. Even when content with your childlessness, it is best to avoid parent holidays. This one would be different, however. We planned a leisurely picnic at a local park, just Isak, David, and me. I sat down on the blanket and opened the picnic basket, and found a Mother's Day card and small gift inside.

When I opened it, time stood still: *Thank you for being my mom and my friend, a cheerleader when I need a fan . . . I love you, Mom.*

Isak went on to say he couldn't have had a better host mom, how thankful he was, and he signed it with a heart followed by *Y.F.H.S.—your favorite host son.*

The tears spilled out, "Thank you," I said. "I love it. I will keep it forever."

And so the word *bittersweet*, written on the napkin his last day of school, is the only one I can think of to describe our year. Without the bitter pill of our loss, the indescribable joy Isak brought would never have entered our lives. The birth mom had needed our support but not our home for her baby. She had grown to become a mother herself. Now Isak's brown eyes stare back at me, emotional and full, his heart near to bursting. I hold the emotion with him, so he will not have to carry it alone.

Isak and I have a song I would play right outside his bedroom door on special days. He has requested it for his last day, and so it rings out, *"Good morning to you!"* With both heaviness and excitement, we scurry through the day, packing too many things into too few bags. After holding him tightly at the airport, I hug him again and let go. It will be at least a week before the pain becomes bearable.

Five days later, we have a Skype video call with his parents, with Isak sandwiched in the middle of them.

"Thank you for everything you did for our son," they say. "When are you coming to our home for a visit? We have a beautiful countryside to show you!"

How can one be related to people four thousand miles away that do not share your language or culture? And yet, we are now, forever.

Isak left nearly five months ago. Before he left, I asked him if he would stay in touch.

He looked at me incredulously, "Who do you think I am? You are stuck with me now."

Just when I think our Skype conversation is about to end, I often hear: "Wait! I have more good news to share!"

I am only too happy to listen.

■ PRAYER

Father, though we still don't understand your ways, we have been touched by the improbable healing in our hearts. Thank you for showing us that love is always a good idea, and that we are coworkers in writing the story of redemption you are telling through our lives. Amen.

■ WRITING PROMPT

What bittersweet event or loss in your life has most impacted you? Write an imaginative piece about what your story of redemption looks like.

My Nonna
by Terri Kraus

Strength. Courage. Endurance.

These were the attributes of my maternal grandmother.

That's what I think of when I remember her.

Even her name, Pierina, means "made of stone." So lovely, so fitting, but she was much more than just strong and brave and persevering. She was a true survivor and a woman of great faith. Hers was not an easy journey, and that journey continues to speak into my life and inspire me decades later; and it always will.

Her story begins in post–World War I Italy, when times were hard. After only a few months of marriage, she became pregnant, and soon after that, her husband, my grandfather, sailed for America seeking a better life for his family. She delivered her first child—a daughter—with her husband thousands of miles away. Her baby was nearly killed in a tragic accident, and it left her severely burned on her face, neck, and upper body. When my grandfather called for his wife a short time later, she traveled across the Atlantic to an unknown place with her weak and scarred firstborn in her arms. Years later, she found a dynamic faith, and because of it she suffered religious persecution by family, friends, and, most hurtful of all, her own husband. She weathered seasons of loneliness and want and suffered a permanent illness—yet her steadfast devotion to the Lord never wavered.

One of the deepest joys of my life was visiting the little northern Italian village named Arola, in the province of Ascoli Piceno, in the region called Le Marche, high up in the Apennine Mountains at the end of a twisting, turning, one-lane road, nestled among centuries-old olive groves—less than a morning's walk from the Adriatic Sea. There, my grandparents, and their parents and grandparents before them, were born, grew up, and cultivated olives. Like most in the village, they married young. And like many after the Great War, they emigrated to America. The village is still much as it was a hundred years ago or more; the same gnarled and shimmery olive trees endure. As if on cue, they were in full bloom for my first visit. A short, steep lane, bordered by glorious tangles of fragrant herbs and wildflowers, connects the rustic stone farmhouses of my grandparents' two families. The open ground floors house livestock; there are cellars in which hunks of homemade prosciutto are hung to dry, and cloth-wrapped wheels of cheese are stored in underground pits to age.

Between these farmhouses stands a small, ivy-covered house built of ancient, mellowed stone with colorful green shutters. Now empty, it is where my grandparents lived as newlyweds. How full my heart felt as I first unlocked that time-worn wooden door and walked over that threshold, my childhood longing at last fulfilled! I pictured them as a young couple in the first blush of matrimony, with all their modest hopes and dreams—before their separate journeys across a wide ocean to a strange land where all was unknown. Within those aged walls, did they speak of their doubts and fears as they prepared to leave their homeland and the safe cloister of their village? This was the only place they'd ever known, and from which they had never ventured more than a mile or two. What kind of courage did that require? Would they ever see their parents and siblings again? What words did they use to comfort and reassure one another? I imagined my Nonna, sitting on a hand-hewn, three-legged stool, stirring a pot of savory tomato *ragù* as my grandfather stoked the fire. I could even hear the crackling of the firewood, smell the pungent wood smoke.

But life for my grandmother would be much different than on that bucolic olive farm between the mountains and the sea. Pierina and her baby endured a long, difficult, and solitary voyage from Genoa,

Italy, to Ellis Island on the ship *Cristoforo Colombo* in 1921, and then made their way by train to Chicago. There was a growing immigrant community west of the city. There, she joined her hardworking husband and settled in among in-laws and extended family. She was soon the mother of three daughters. Life during the Great Depression was difficult. Her heart ached with longing for her parents and the farm. The quiet, idyllic rural life she knew in her early years became a distant memory, and she learned to make do with very little in their rented home. It was an aging Victorian that had seen better days, on a busy street, but it was always spotless. They had to take in boarders—common in those days—to make ends meet. Her days were long and wearying.

Then her life changed. She was invited to a prayer meeting in the home of a friend and was introduced to a new spiritual reality—a transformational life she'd never thought possible—through a personal, intimate, and vibrant relationship with Jesus Christ. But the joy of the Lord she would come to know came at a great price. She was shunned by her husband. Her in-laws and extended family saw her newfound faith as an insult to their old-world religious beliefs and traditions. Some even thought she was deranged. Her prayer time would be a time to hide—behind the locked door of the bathroom, or in the damp, low-ceilinged basement adding coal to the furnace or doing laundry at the washboard. If my grandfather caught her reading God's Word, he would snatch the Bible out of her hands and destroy it—tear it up or burn it. The precious fellowship she and her daughters enjoyed at a tiny, storefront mission church was done secretly—necessary to avoid the hostility of her husband and family.

After a surgical mistake in her midforties, she would greatly suffer physically, every day, for the rest of her life. Yet—yet—she knew the inexplicable peace of God, and her eternal hope was her rock. She remained faithful to the Lord, a bold witness, freely telling anyone she met about this Jesus who had changed her life, blossoming and bearing much fruit. She would generously share what little she had with scores of hungry homeless men who would tap at her door at suppertime. She'd make a place for them at her table, pray for them, and share the good news of the Gospel in broken English. She clung to her faith despite great adversity, found her delight in her Lord and in her home, possessing a supernatural serenity even in her pain. She never failed to give God the glory for everything, and she was never one to complain about her challenges. Like those ancient olive trees, she not only endured—she truly thrived.

Nonna became a young widow in her midfifties, when I was three months old, and lived with our family until her death when I was eight. Her middle daughter, Anna, my mother—who is also a vibrant, godly woman after her mother's heart—willingly and tenderly cared for Nonna's many physical needs. My mother had been raised seeing great forgiveness and unconditional love quietly lived out in difficult family circumstances, and her own sacrificial love and servant's heart are the hallmarks of who she is to me. Nonna's children, grandchildren, and great-grandchildren, and the countless children whom she loved well in her Sunday school classes for decades, would come to faith in Christ through her example and teaching.

My Nonna was the quintessential vision of the little Italian grandma—perpetually wearing an apron, her hair in a bun, small in stature but huge in spirit. My memories of her are of hearing her fervent prayers during her daily devotion time. They were always in Italian, always out loud. I clearly remember the simple worship choruses she sang in that beautiful language as she rolled out sheets of pasta or mounds of biscotti; when she felt up to it, her first desire was always to cook and bake, for to her food equaled love. She smelled of basil and garlic, and I can still vividly recall the simple pleasure of her welcoming me home from school on a chilly Chicago day with a still-warm slice of her incomparable freshly baked, crusty bread slathered with butter. I would be captivated for hours listening to her tell tales of her early life in Arola, and longed to see this magical place where my family's history, and my story, began.

Images from my visit to Arola remain with me, along with a couple of rustic artifacts I found in that little stone house on the lane between the family farms: an old, tarnished, green olive-oil tin and a battered olive strainer of wood and rusted metal. I was delighted to take these home with me to America. They are of little material value as antiques, but how I treasure them and prominently display them in my home, because they take me back to that village in the olive groves and connect me with that place, frozen in time. They remind me of my rich spiritual heritage and are priceless symbols of the enduring olive trees, with their incredible longevity, strength, and fruitfulness. They have become a cherished metaphor for my grandmother's life—poured out and sifted, yet useful, remaining—which still inspires me.

When, in the struggles of my life, I become short on courage, charity, peace, and joy, I remember my Nonna, now wholly healed within that great cloud of witnesses. I hope to pass on to my own child the seed of faithfulness that was planted in my mother by my Nonna, the first Christ-follower in my family, and which has been planted in me by my mother, and which I pray will continually grow—a legacy worthy of these remarkable women of God. For from them I have learned, and I believe to my core, that there is nothing—nothing— that brings God greater glory than to see one of his own face suffering and hardship with joy, hope, and peace.

Thank you, Nonna. Thank you, God.

■ PRAYER

Sovereign God, I acknowledge that, on my own, living a Christian life is not possible. I need the power of the Holy Spirit, which you promised to freely give me. I long for it, Father. I ask that you help me each day to live more fully into the abundant life you offer and provide, even in times of suffering. It is what my hungry soul wants and needs. In this chaotic world, may I be healed where I am broken, may I be enveloped in your peace, and may I reflect your great love. Enable me to pass these treasures on to those who come after me. Thank you. In the name of Jesus Christ, our Lord. Amen.

■ WRITING PROMPT

Describe a strong and influential woman in your life.

The Secret to Bloom
by Aleah Marsden

I turn right off the main road, make a sharp left down the paved driveway, being especially careful as I'm in my borrowed father-in-law's truck. Ahead of me the house is made of the same white stone that apparently is used all over Austin, Texas. The rough texture gives the feel that even these custom developments have somehow sprung up organically next to the bluebells lining the walk. The morning light is radiant, the air chilly but holding the promise of a gorgeous, warm afternoon.

Truth is, I've been imagining this visit for a couple of months—since I had the pleasure of being asked to edit the memoir of my friend's father. Diving into someone's life in that way, I had been caught off guard by the intimacy I already felt with these people—to Gene, whose memoir I had edited, and to his wife, Frances. Gene and Frances met at Texas A&M, married in 1954, lived on love and green tomatoes in those early years, raised four kids, and moved what seemed to me at least a dozen times. I clung to every word of the story unfolding in front of me, as I made my nitpicky edits for proper tense and asked for elaboration in other places. I could see my family—my husband, the kids, and me—in many places. I wondered how our own story will look one day when we reflect back, more behind us than ahead.

Though Gene was the protagonist in the pages, I couldn't help but be drawn to his vivacious wife. Whenever his job as a chemical engineer uprooted the family, she dutifully packed, pulled up roots, and replanted herself in a new community—sometimes across the country, even as far-flung as Puerto Rico!

I saw a pattern emerge: each time Frances moved, she brought the Gospel with her. For every new context, she found a new opportunity to use her gifts, especially teaching the Bible—often hosting small Bible studies in her living room. While doing this on the second stay in Puerto Rico, Frances recognized her translator's gift for teaching equipped her to take over the study. During a stint in Connecticut, she founded a Bible Study Fellowship (BSF) group and served it faithfully as a teaching leader for twelve years as the class grew to over 150 women.

Frances was stealing the story. I found myself eager to take time away from my laptop so I could sit at the feet of this wise teacher. Gene's deep affection and admiration were obvious. I could feel the way he swelled with pride over her accomplishments, even while listing his own noteworthy work almost as an aside. I began to have a deep longing to meet this woman who had unearthed a secret for which I had been hunting most of my adult life: how to bloom.

I've lived in the same, sleepy northern California suburb for twenty-eight years—since I was four. It is not out of the ordinary for me to run into someone at Target whom I've known since elementary school. My roots into my community run deep, but long roots don't ensure vibrant blossoms. I've spent much of my life timidly attempting to discern what type of exotic plant I must be—no college education, married young, four kids, an introvert who loves public speaking, a heart rent by seemingly competing desires. In my digging, I have wondered if perhaps this domestic soil lacks some key nutrient essential to my flourishing.

The more I read, the more in awe I was of this couple's faithfulness. When I realized they lived in Austin and that I would be out that way to attend the IF:Gathering, I started praying for the courage to ask if I could stop in. Meeting new people is hard for me, asking something of new people is harder, and following through is hardest. My longing to meet Frances trumped my fear of looking foolish, but before I even had a chance to ask, Gene e-mailed with an open invitation for me to visit anytime. He offered before he even knew I would be in the area and able to take him up on it.

Walking up to the crimson double doors flanked by huge windows, I smiled at the strange sensation of feeling familiarity with a building I was seeing for the first time. I knew they had built it as their dream retirement home—the location best suited to spending their remaining years, where they could golf and slow down and finally settle.

It was only months before when Gene had realized he just wasn't cut out for retirement. Instead they would rent the house, and he and Frances would pursue a call they both felt for missionary work. I remember nearly spitting out my coffee as I edited this section of the manuscript. I could not make this up. Instead of basking in the comfort of their custom home outside Austin, Gene and Frances chose to spend their golden years teaching English in Mozambique.

I was beginning to wonder if perhaps the secret to blooming was in the uprooting and replanting. Of course! Frances's secret must be in her appetite for adventure. Maybe exotic plants require exotic soil. I was enraptured and more than a little jealous. If only I had wander-means to match my wanderlust, then I would surely blossom as well.

I timidly tap on the large door, thinking about why Gene and Frances had been forced to return to Austin.

⁂

Trying to hide the tears on my cheeks while sitting in a coffee shop on a drizzly December afternoon, I learned that Frances had been diagnosed with Huntington's disease. I immediately googled it and learned that Huntington's disease affects muscle coordination and leads to mental decline and behavioral issues. *Oh, Lord, not Frances.* I shot up an arrow of a prayer, even knowing I was reading this years after the fact. My eyes skimmed across the pages, knowing I would have to go back over and edit but unable to stop. As Frances's condition deteriorated, their daughters came to Mozambique to help them back to Austin.

They returned home—where I now stood on the marble front stoop, a little nervous about meeting these people I had come to love without having ever met.

⁂

It's always helpful to bring along an extrovert for these situations—and my sweet friend Karina had agreed to join me for this visit. Gene opens the front door, hugs us both, and shows us into the high-ceilinged living room. Windows lining the back of the room bathe every surface in natural light, the décor a homage to their world travels.

I am relieved to see Frances sitting in an armchair facing us. I hadn't known what to expect and was too shy to ask beforehand. She smiles at me and shows me the pillow in her lap with a cherubic picture of a big-eyed baby looking up at us: her great-granddaughter. We exchange a quick embrace before Gene leads Karina and me out to the back patio to take in the sweeping views of Texas hill country.

Gene's quick wit and easy laugh make me feel at home instantly. Before we have left the back porch, he is already inviting me and my entire family out to visit. He introduces us to Frances's in-home caretaker as we settle onto the couches in the living room. He never speaks as if Frances isn't sitting there, as some people are inclined to do around persons with disabilities, but frequently defers to her. She answers, her voice somewhat slurred, in single words or short sentences or big grins with vigorous nods. Her dark eyes are alert.

Gene jovially leads us into the kitchen, warning us, "I made us a breakfast casserole. My first one. Now, don't feel obligated to eat it. It might not be edible. Maybe just eat the sausage out of it or something." He tells us Frances and the home-care worker had been laughing watching him prepare it. The table is already set with fruit, juice, coffee, and assorted baked goods. I feel a pang of guilt that he would go to such trouble, but am assuaged seeing the joy with which he serves.

As we chat over our (totally edible) casserole, conversation turns to Frances's condition. It has become too hard to attend church, so they watch online. Traveling, other than doctor's visits, is over. Frances shifts in her chair, and Gene points out that sitting upright is painful and exhausting. "I'm alright," Frances immediately chimes in, smiling, meeting Gene's appraising glance. Her caretaker points out that a symptom of Huntington's disease can be large personality changes; many people become angry and agitated, understandably overwhelmed and frustrated with their degenerative situation, but not Frances. The caretaker smiles at her with awe and says, "She's still so gentle. So worried about others. More concerned with everyone else than herself."

Plates are cleared, and conversations dissipate. Karina follows Gene into the kitchen, and Frances's caretaker goes to set up what she will need to help Frances into bed. I get out of my seat, torn between needing to leave and needing to talk to Frances, who has remained at the table. Awkwardly, shyly, I approach her, squatting down so we are at eye level. What is her secret? To an untrained eye, the flower of her life would appear to be wilting, but I have witnessed over brunch how each gentle petal that falls is a blessing to the person who receives it.

My words are failing me while my mind races. I feel our moment too quickly passing, but what do you say when you find yourself in the presence of a saint? "Thank you," I whisper. "You inspire me." She reaches out and takes my face in both her soft, slightly contorted hands. Light streams in the large window behind me, while her bright eyes lock on mine and she smiles. There are no words, only blessing.

A few months have passed since that visit. Bored and melting in the sweltering southern California heat, I wait in the longest line we have endured on this Disneyland trip, to board Space Mountain. My phone buzzes in my back pocket, a welcome distraction to the monotony. I flick open an e-mail from Gene:

Dear ones,

My loving wife left this earth to be with her Savior at 7AM this morning, Monday, April 27, 2015. Frances was in her bed in our home and very peaceful while surrounded by her three children and me, when she breathed her last. I know that Frances is having a great time with her Savior and with all the loved ones who have gone ahead, but my life will not be the same without her. She was simply put, the best wife ever.

I gasp, the wind knocked out of me. The line inches forward as if no one has noticed.

I learned from Frances that it is neither the soil of our circumstance nor our groundbreaking gifts that bring flourishing. Rather, it is the nourishment received from orienting ourselves to the sun that produces the most breathtaking blooms. I imagine her face now, radiant in the reflected glory of her Savior, smiling with understanding.

Saint Frances: my patron saint of blooming where you're planted.

■ PRAYER

Caring Father, tend to the fertile soil of my soul, and show me how I can join you in this good work. Bring my life to bloom in season, and help me trust your perfect timing. Amen.

■ WRITING PROMPT

Write about one small way you have reoriented yourself or could reorient yourself to the Source of flourishing.

The Story of a Voice
by Linda MacKillop

"Child," said the Lion, "I am telling you your story, not hers.
No one is told any story but their own."
—C. S. Lewis, *The Horse and His Boy*[15]

A coffee mug appeared in my home when I was a little girl. "Boss," the bold lettering read across the porcelain front. When I was eight years old and angry, my siblings claimed the mug was for little, innocent, blonde-haired, blue-eyed me. I threw a temper tantrum. They saw me as a little sister who insisted on everyone's obedience to her wishes. I *demanded* they believe I wasn't a *boss*. Finally, everyone laughed and admitted the mug had been given to my grandfather.

I want to tell you a story. The story of the forming of a voice. It begins with that young, overly confident, bossy girl misusing her voice; then she loses her voice to passive behavior; finally she discovers a new, redeemed one.

This is the story of how a troubled home with hollering voices and projectiles shattering on solid walls stifled a voice and slowly disintegrated a family. Wide-eyed and trembling in our beds at night while adults screamed unthinkable things to each other, my siblings and I learned how voices change after overindulgence in drink. We begged our adults to replace the vodka bottles with adult-like behavior, and we were ignored—our young voices retreated inside us.

The marriage ended within a decade.

This once bossy girl grew into a sulking, silent teenager. While the boys' voices around me lowered in range due to testosterone, my voice practically disappeared—self-assurance was replaced with devastating passivity. I entered a season of rebellion toward family and teachers—it was the sixties and seventies, after all. Rebellion was in the air we breathed, along with smoke of all kinds. I lost my voice even in situations where I most needed to say *no*. I followed along, saying hello to a me who never refused anything offered, no matter how harmful and degrading. As my voice vanished, my shame increased.

I became silent in classes, in groups, and around friends. One night as I sat on my bed with the sea air wafting in through my open window, inspiration struck. A poem formed when my pen touched the crisp page of my journal. After finishing my writing, I reread the words to find I had written a surprising poem about acceptance, a topic unfamiliar to me. No one in my family or school or Sunday school ever talked about *acceptance.*

Later in life I would replace *acceptance* with *surrender to God*, but in that moment, words penned by me taught me.

I wondered at this inspired poem's arrival. It ignited hope for a different life built around honing a talent; I began to dream of going to college and studying creative writing. Maybe I had words worth sharing? Maybe I could get away from my troubled friends and start over? I began to love writing because writing felt like an expression of love—as if some far-off place or Person was calling to me.

My father loved my pursuit of writing, as he harbored secret regrets that he hadn't been able to do creative work. He and my mother began a family at a young age, forcing him to take an unsatisfying job in retail. He gave me an IBM electric typewriter when I graduated from high school with a note saying, "Write stories and publish them!"

Just as I was starting to heal from a tumultuous childhood, an event devastated my voice. At nineteen, I had made it to college in one piece after taking a year off to get the money together to pay my own way. Arriving at Florida State like an aged woman weary of irresponsible living, I looked forward to a new season of learning the craft of writing and delving into books.

But on Thanksgiving night of my first semester, after an argument with my boyfriend late at night, disoriented and intoxicated, I jumped out of his truck. Unbeknownst to me, he had taken a shortcut through an extremely dangerous part of town. Within seconds of my boots hitting the sidewalk, four young men approached me. They picked me up, silenced my screams with their hands over my mouth, and carried me to an abandoned house several streets away.

In the time it took for my boyfriend to drive to the next stoplight and return for me, I was gone.

Inside a back bedroom of an empty bungalow, unable to freely leave, I frantically examined my options. My only escape routes seemed to be breaking through the barrier at the door or crashing through the window. I considered risking the results of splintered glass all over my body, until I realized all that was outside the window was another abandoned house. No one was around to save me.

So this is how my life will end—my mind raced with my foolish choices and my years of silence toward my family and friends. I had wasted my brief nineteen years on earth, and never told anyone I loved them.

I survived thanks to an old ploy I'd used when my brothers and I would wrestle. I pretended I was dead. No matter what violent, degrading assaults my attackers inflicted, I refused to respond. Believing they had killed me, the attackers ran away, but not until wishing out loud that they had brought knives to finish me off. The next morning the police officer found a screwdriver hidden from sight in the corner of the room when they took me back to the crime scene. If one of my attackers had bumped against the metal of the screwdriver with his shoe, I am convinced they would have used it to end my life in that disgusting room.

For You are my lamp, O Lord;
And the Lord illumines my darkness.
—2 Samuel 22:29 (NASB)

Thankfully my story did not end there. It was a horrible and dark chapter. Although I didn't find God during the rape, and viewed all of life through that violent and nearly fatal lens for my remaining college years, I did find God eventually *because* of the rape.

Unless you've experienced an assault such as this, it can be hard to understand the winding path of pain and healing. But my story reflects that of many others who have known this path—*God rescued me from myself as a result of my experience.* You can't tussle with death, know evil, and stare fear straight in the face and not be transformed. It gave me a new passion for life.

My voice nearly being snuffed out altogether changed my voice.

After the assault, when I returned to campus, my ears perked up to the abundant discussions about God. I was hungry for this Person who had been calling me my whole life. I began to express affection to others. The Great Hound of Heaven hunted me down through bold people telling me—verbally and in writing—of Christ's existence, and my soul responded, leading me into a church after graduation. Meeting with the pastor, I told him of my desire to be a Christian. He responded, "Other people brought you to this place. I am honored to pray with you." And my entire world and all of my relationships changed after this meeting.

My family responded negatively to the new *me*. My relationships with my parents grew distant. Struggling with severe depression, my father moved far away without staying in touch. My relationship with my mother grew increasingly toxic and unhealthy, eventually leading to my painful decision to remain estranged from her indefinitely. I would learn of her death by throat cancer through a post on Facebook.

My writing hit a speed bump as all these shattered life-story details caused me to feel inadequate as a storyteller. How could someone like me offer wise words to anyone? Shame about events in my past grew into shame about my story. Instead of awards, accolades, and accomplishments, my life seemed only to boast of failures. I retreated again.

But this is also a story of what happens when a woman with a tremulous voice waits on God.

During those early years as a believer, I entered into a long season of listening and learning, allowing time to be my instructor, helping me to process my experiences from God's perspective. I would allow my writer's voice time to grow in substance before displaying my transformation to others. Meanwhile, I married a wonderful man, and sons began appearing. Writing remained in the background, though the desire and quiet sense of calling never left me.

When my four sons shuffled off to school, I began taking writing classes. But all of my stories—then and now—seemed so dark. When you are lugging heavy shame and mess on your crippled back, your writing reflects it. Who wants to hear about such ugliness?

But along the way, other writers encouraged me by owning their stories and courageously telling them. I began to discover the sound of my writing voice and the look of my audience, which resembled me in so many ways. I chose to write unashamedly about ugly stories—mine and those of others. For many years I discounted God's work in my life and still saw the reflection of that shame-filled, troubled girl looking back at me from the page. She caused me to write sideways sometimes, coming at truth from an angle. I was less bold and less direct than others who confidently shared their positions, opinions, politics—their lives.

I found fiction writing and discovered that it allows me to step back and speak with enough distance between the reader and me. The best part? I can change endings. In my novel *Try Again Farm*, the family heals. The cantankerous old woman finds redemption, asks for forgiveness, and learns to step out of isolation to give to others. In my middle-grade novel *Hotel, Oscar, Mike, Echo,* someone rescues the troubled child—providing a home to the homeless, peace to the shamed, hope to the hopeless.

So this is the story of my voice: part stubborn and bossy, part troubled teen who was violated and who nearly lost her life before encountering the Most High God, who used an exceedingly hard road to transform me.

This is about how all my experiences, privileges, depravations, personality traits, backgrounds, accomplishments, and failures appear in my writing, as my unique voice—as unique as a thumbprint, as unique as a life. No one else writes with my voice.

Most importantly, this is the praiseworthy story of many, many voices joined together in one grand conversation, which resulted in my redemption and will result in the redemption of others. An army of witnesses, all taking part in a glorious dialogue through printed and spoken words—these healing voices and stories saturated my soul. Today, they honor me with a humbling invitation to add my shaking, trembling, nervous voice to the rising chorus beckoning us all home.

PRAYER

Heavenly Father, you who number our days, thank you for this opportunity to review your role in my life. Please give me eyes to see how my past forms and blossoms me into a person you can use. Grow me into a woman who speaks with hope to others from my unique life experiences. In Jesus's name. Amen.

WRITING PROMPT

Describe an experience in your life that formed your voice and blossomed you into a person God can use to transform your own story as well as those of others.

A Fine Day for You to Be God
by Ronne Rock

What does true hope look like when shame fills the streets and threatens the lives of all it meets? Does hope exist at all?

I've been to so many countries where life is eked out in drops like sweat. If I close my eyes, I can see the arch-backed men on the side of the road carrying coffee beans they've plucked from the scrub in Guatemala, and the disease-ridden mothers struggling to raise wide-eyed and wondering children in precariously perched huts in India. But there's something about the Kayole Matopeni slum of Nairobi, Kenya—a shame that crawls through the streets and latches on without regard to age or ability. Less than five miles away, high-rise apartments and luxury hotels invite businesses to consider Kenya for economic development.

No one considers the slum.

The constant metallic din of hammers chipping away at stone fills the air. From dawn until dusk, mommas bend low and break rocks in the stifling heat and sudden rains. The work done to make others wealthy rarely provides enough to keep food on the table for the families living in metal shanties and cinder-block cells.

Across a river of waste, the Kenyan Army conducts military drills with live rounds. Wayward shots go ignored in this place where lives are lived in obscurity. The sewage of the entire city snakes through the center of the eastern Nairobi slum; trash dances in the streets in search of a resting place.

I had come to Kenya with a picture of slums painted in my mind— late-night infomercial images of desolation put on display for all to see.

And what my eyes saw confirmed the pain. But standing on the streets of Kayole Matopeni, I found something unexpected.

All around me, everyday life moved in tattered, high-walled miniature.

People live and die, work and rest, buy and sell and trade. Humanity is welcomed and lost. Parents go to work and children go to school and teenagers dream of a life that's bigger. Brooms are kept in quiet corners to sweep away the dust that returns and returns.

It was here in the dust that we found her home—the oldest of three siblings. Alice, the school director, had invited all three to attend school after watching them peek day after day through the iron gates that guard the entryway. Dhana led the way to the rusted, corrugated metal door to her home and moved the rock that kept it closed.

Inside, two dogs sniffed a frightened welcome in the mud-and-muck courtyard where a cow had been. Briefly, it had been a better time in the children's lives, a time when milk could be drunk and sold for a little food money. Then the cow was stolen. The courtyard felt ravaged. A grandmother staying with the family fled for higher ground.

And so it was just Dhana and her two brothers most hours of the day, there in the mud and the muck.

She quietly observed us, wondering what we would say about this place—about her. The door to her home was open, revealing one bed for everyone. There was no room for anything or anyone else, no room to invite guests, no room to have a seat and talk. But now here were guests, pale ghosts in clothes with no stains or tears, quietly taking in every small detail.

"Your home, it is so very beautiful."

She looked with curious eyes and smiled, then stood a little taller in the doorway.

"It really is lovely."

She smiled again, and watched each face intently as the ghosts prayed for her, prayed for her home, and prayed for the day there would be no need.

Stepping through the rusted metal outer door, we began our journey back to the noise and security of a school that had become the young girl's sanctuary and sustenance. Through a field of debris, a woman walked toward us, eyes like flint.

Alice recognized her. "Oh friends, this is Nzuri. She is the mother."

She didn't know why she felt the urgency to leave her work and walk across the slum. But Nzuri was here now, here with us. She stood there, resilient in the smog and dirt. I recognized the smell of the dump—of waste and chemicals and fire.

I have held the hands of the people of the Ravine in Guatemala so many times, but never have I known someone like Nzuri. Her labor had become her identity—pants shredded, boots warped, shirt like sandpaper, flies swarming skin embedded with refuse. The dump had tied itself around her.

And yet, she stood resolutely before us. I could hear the hiss of shame around her. And yet it could not touch her.

Nzuri shared her story.

From sunrise to starlight, stooped over debris, she digs. Her hands swollen and deformed from sifting, she hopes to find food scraps in the trash—she can sell them to the lucky ones who have a goat or pig. A bucket of scraps earns a few cents. On the best of days, Nzuri might make five dollars. On the rest of days, she will be fortunate to bring home a dollar.

A dollar. For a mom and three children.

I can't remember the last time I really ached—you know, one of those deep, overwhelming, "catch your breath in your throat" aches that lives somewhere between a sigh and a scream. The day before, walking the sewage-lined paths that mocked streets in the Mathare slums, I felt the sorrowful hope of what my best friend and I had coined the "beautiful-awful" of this very fragile life. Like a tender flower pushing its way through cracks in concrete. It was the same hope I had seen bloom in so many other places—abandoned churches in Romanian villages and forgotten streets in poverty-stricken Texas neighborhoods. I had come to expect the hope, always encouraging others to look deeply for it when pity threatened to choke. I ached for Nzuri. I ached for hope to bloom in her life.

My hands felt so empty. I wanted to snatch her from the slum and be her safekeeping, to take away all longing and to make life easy and carefree. A stumbling prayer rattled in my head. *It would be a good day for You to show Yourself strong. It would be a fine day for You to rescue and save. It would be a fine day for You to be God.*

We listened as she gave thanks for the education of her children. She shared her dream that their lives would be better. We asked if we might pray.

Alice smiled and looked at our group. "You do not ask to pray in Kenya. You ask *how* you might pray here. We will pray Heaven down today!"

Nzuri's eyes glistened with tears as she responded. "We need God's will to be done. Pray for it to be well with my family."

I looked around at the others who were listening, trying to make sense of the prayer that made no demands, contained no self-pity. Simply, *pray for it to be well.*

Hands reached for hands. She hesitated and then held hers out. Would anyone reach back? Toward hands deformed and dirty.

Hands reached for hands; hers completed the circle.

There was silence, then her hushed voice fought through the tears now streaming.

"I need Jesus."

There, on the street holding hands with strangers, Eternity met us all. Eternity spoke its response.

Shame could not touch her because hope had bloomed in her.

We stood side by side, stripped of all but who we were. In me, the ache had overwhelmed the hope, and I wanted to save and fix and take away pain so there would be no more crumbling—I silently screamed at God to do something, to show up and make things right.

All the while, he was there.

In the everyday life, in the stooping and shame—he is there.

The woman in sandpaper shirt and shredded pants became the gentle reminder of true hope. She hadn't asked for salvation from her days. She had asked for salvation in them.

I held Nzuri tightly. With tears streaming down my face, her prayers became mine. God's will. God's grace. God's mercy.

One word—Jesus.

We all felt hope's bloom.

■ PRAYER

One word: Jesus. We need this reminder each day, Lord. Keep our hearts aching, Lord. Let the ache never choke out the hope that is always waiting to bloom in our lives. Let our prayer always be "God's will, God's grace, God's mercy." With Isaiah we pray:

I celebrate and shout
because of my LORD God.
His saving power and justice
are the very clothes I wear.
They are more beautiful
than the jewelry worn
by a bride or a groom.
The LORD will bring about
justice and praise
in every nation on earth,

like flowers blooming
in a garden.
—Isaiah 61:10–11 (CEV)
Amen.

■ WRITING PROMPT

How could you commune with and serve the desperate in your community? Describe where you have seen Eternity break into your world.

The Advent of Hope
by Tammy Perlmutter

On the advent of antiquity
I AM
brought into being
Crows, chrysanthemums, caterpillars, clouds—
Creating form and function
Facets and features out
Of nothing.
It was infinitely more than nothing
That brought calm out of chaos and
Breath into being
Mind into matter
Spirit into soul
People into promise

Love into life
Love that gives and graces and generates
Three times as much love
A trinity of capacity
Expanding dimension and scope
A magnitude of out-of-proportion love
A *bigger on the inside* kind of love
That defies classification, method,
Logic, sense, reason,
Gravity even
When Love came down
And brought us
Hope

The thing with more than just feathers
But hands feet heart
The thing becoming a Who
Becoming a He
Who would rescue our
Deep, dark hearts
From hurt and hate and hell
Harnessing heaven
Hijacking history

To give us haters and us hurters
Hope
And a future,
Hope
In a He who would usher in
Hope
In the face of fear and failure and falsehood,
This swaddled son
The favored One
Who heaps favor on us
To be for us
The friend
The father
The generous benefactor
Of all good things
Given by God
In his great mercy
Granting us more than we could
Hope
Or expect
From He who is more than we deserve
More than we can imagine

More than we can comprehend
Estimate
Calculate
Correlate
Communicate
This communion
State of this union
Of faith and hope and love
This newborn stranger,
This hope in a manger
This hope of Israel
The hope of their fathers
The hope of the poor
Hope of human hearts
The hope of all the ends of the earth

This hope of salvation
Of all who need saving
All who are straining
To receive
Struggling
To believe
In a
Hope
That
Does not
Disappoint.

■ PRAYER

Father God, I thank you for being my rock and fortress, strong tower and deliverer, and my last standing hope when I am tempted to despair. Holy Spirit, infuse my heart with strength to push past fears, and peace in order to be a source of comfort and encouragement to others. Jesus, thank you for being the ultimate Creator and for all you are doing and will do in my life. Amen.

■ WRITING PROMPT

What is God creating out of your nothing?

This Is What It Costs
by Lara Krupicka

dump the silverware onto my kitchen island counter in a clattering pile. Crumbs and dust fall out atop forks and knives. After giving a few swipes with a damp dishcloth to the bottom of the now-empty drawer, I slide it back in place. It gives a satisfying hollow slam.

Across the kitchen I slip out another drawer where my husband has stored dishcloths and towels. A quick tip, and the contents fall to my kitchen table. I repeat the process with several more drawers before stepping back to survey my progress.

It's a mess. Piles everywhere, with crumbs and paper scraps and other detritus of everyday living silted among them. I'm buoyed by the sight, energized to complete the transformation. I need to finish this project. It is my first step in reclaiming myself.

Thirteen years prior, my husband and I had moved into another house—our first house, where we would spend five years. It was small and in need of repairs and updates. But love and youthfulness naively marched us forward. We tore out carpeting and had the hardwood floors refinished. We painted. We plunged into the world of do-it-yourselfers and quickly learned we needed the advice of those more experienced in home repairs.

In the process I learned that there was a "right way" and a "wrong way" for almost everything. "It's easier to trim in a wall if you fan the bristles this way," my mother-in-law would explain.

"Why are you hunched over like that?" my husband asked as I helped him feed electrical wire. "Kneel. You'll save your back."

Colors for finishes and paints came with opinions and decisions. "That one won't go with the existing trim," someone would say. "Don't you think that's too bright?" another would suggest.

I became overwhelmed by the responsibilities of home ownership and all the new things to learn. Innocent questions posed by well-intentioned family members made me doubt myself, doubt whether my ideas were worthwhile, and whether my plans for completing various tasks were valid.

And then we had a baby. Suddenly it was no longer just family offering advice and telling me what I was doing wrong. Strangers would give me disapproving looks when my baby cried during a supermarket outing. Friends would warn me of all the ways my baby could come to harm, like being fed honey too young, or sleeping on her stomach.

My self-doubt grew. And my lifelong desire to please others expanded with it. In a few years there were two children with a third on the way. Now I planned meals around not only what my husband liked but also what would tempt the palates of little kids. I chose outings based on what would entertain our girls, dreading the noise and chaos of places like the children's museum, yet gritting my teeth for their benefit.

By the time we moved to our second and current house—a bigger one to fit a family of five—the range of decisions in my control had shrunk dramatically. My husband drew up a schematic of how he wanted the kitchen laid out. For maximum efficiency, he explained. Bowls and plates here. Cups there. Silverware by the sink for ease of putting away from the dishwasher. Dishtowels next to the stove. I looked it over and agreed it was the epitome of kitchen efficiency. Never mind that I would be the one spending the most time in the kitchen. We organized it by his plan.

And there it is: I am gone, lost to what others want. To the desire to please and keep peace. Lost down a deep well of trying hard not to want what I want, not to do what I want to do. But I don't notice the loss. In my mind I am doing what a "good" wife and a "good" mother does.

Two years later, we sit at the dinner table when the topic of favorites comes up—a topic every kid loves to explore. We take turns talking about what we like.

"What is my favorite color? That's easy," I respond. "Blue." And in truth it is. I have loved blue in all varieties since I was a young girl. My current preference? Teal.

And then the question, "What's your favorite food?" I don't have an answer. So I shrug it off. After all, I like lots of food. I'm not picky. But my girls press me to pick a favorite. The mashed potatoes I am eating suddenly stick in my throat, and an itch forms in the middle of my back. Finally, I spit out a response: "Chinese food." I think it's the right answer, but even as I say it I doubt myself.

My girls nod their approval, three little heads bobbing over their plates of meatloaf and mashed potatoes. The itch subsides, and my heartbeat settles. Until the oldest prompts another round of discussion. "What is your favorite place?"

Again, I realize that I don't know. What am I supposed to answer? I think. What is the right answer?

The same panic arises in me over decisions big and small every day. "What movie do you want to watch?" my husband asks. "Whatever you choose," I answer. My default mode. Ordering at a restaurant paralyzes me—I go online and read menus ahead of time, hoping it will help me be prepared. It never does. And so I ask around the table, "What are you getting?" I let others show me the correct dish to order.

Avoid deciding. Then you can't be wrong.

My mother sees. And she won't let me get away with it any longer.

"Where is that stubborn girl I raised?" she asks one day as I sit alone at her kitchen counter, telling her of a decision I'm having a hard time making. "Where is the girl who traipsed off to Russia on her own? Who knew what she wanted and where she was going?"

I'm stunned into silence. The next morning I stand in my shower and sob. I am sad and I am scared at what I have done. I have paid the price for my choice not to decide for myself—and the price is me. I am left empty-handed and empty-souled. And the peace I tried to buy with people-pleasing did not endure. Passing decisions off to others whom I believed were better qualified to get it right—best, most efficient— didn't gain me happiness. Instead, it left a hole.

This is what it costs to forget that God asks us to aim for his pleasure and not that of others. So I have to learn again. My self, my identity, is too much to pay for the happiness of others. And the pleasure of the One who made me has already been paid for (if it even could be bought), by his Son.

A mentor suggests an action that will allow me to take back my voice and my place in making decisions for myself and my family. Rearrange the kitchen to suit my process. Not my husband's "efficient" arrangement, but one that I like. And so, I am making another mess, this one external to match the mess inside. With each drawer emptied, I am filled with strength and confidence.

My opinions matter. My decisions are valid. My way doesn't have to be wrong so that others can be right. Making choices doesn't have to be scary. And what I prefer sometimes just might be as good for my kids and my husband as what they would choose.

After all, Paul tells the Philippians to look out not only for their own interests but also for the interests of others. It doesn't have to mean neglecting myself.

I place the neatly arranged silverware in a drawer beside the table. Stacks of folded towels and dishcloths go into a spot by the fridge.

Over the years my identity had fallen further and further down that well of people-pleasing. But now, with God's help, I am reeling it back up. I'm honoring him by honoring who he created me to be—one rearranged kitchen drawer at a time.

■ PRAYER

Father God, thank you for creating me uniquely as your image bearer. Help me to appreciate that the world needs me to be wholly myself in order to know you better. Give me an eagerness to serve others that is not overcome by a faulty sense of self. Forgive me for the times that I put pleasing others over pleasing you. Help me listen to you more urgently when I have a hard time making a decision, knowing that your opinion of me will never waver because of what Jesus did for me and my sins on the cross. Amen.

■ WRITING PROMPT

What are the limitations, either real or perceived, that keep you from being yourself? Describe what it would look like if you lived your life rooted in God, with an authentic voice blossoming—free to tell your story.

Notes

The Tamarisk by Jen Pollock Michel

1   Wendell Berry, *Jayber Crow* (Berkeley, CA: Counterpoint Press, 2001).

Finding Freedom from Fear by Angie Ryg

2   Trillia J. Newbell, *Fear and Faith: Finding the Peace Your Heart Craves* (Chicago: Moody Publishers, 2015), 35.

3   Robby Gallaty, *Firmly Planted: How to Cultivate a Faith Rooted in Christ* (Nashville, TN: Crossbooks, 2015), 34.

Finding Myself at Fenway by Dorothy Greco

4   Ann Voskamp, *The Broken Way* (Grand Rapids, MI: Zondervan, 2016), 26.

5   Carolyn Custis James, *Malestrom: Manhood Swept into the Currents of a Changing World* (Grand Rapids, MI: Zondervan, 2015), 176.

6   Dorothy Littell Greco, *Making Marriage Beautiful* (Colorado Springs, CO: David C. Cook, 2017), 14.

7   David Benner, *The Gift of Being Yourself* (Downers Grove, IL: InterVarsity Press, 2004), 11.

Firmly Rooted by Peggy Mindrebo

8   T. S. Eliot, *Little Gidding* (Glasgow: Faber and Faber University Press, 1960).

Grief. Sit with It. by Whitney R. Simpson

9   George Eliot, *Middlemarch* (Edinburgh and London: William Blackwood and Sons, 1871–2)

I Am a Desperate Woman by Ashley Hales

10   Christie Purifoy, *Roots and Sky: A Journey Home in Four Seasons* (Grand Rapids, MI: Revell, 2016).

11   Lauren Winner, *Wearing God: Clothing, Fire, Laughter, and Other Over-looked Metaphors for God* (New York: HarperCollins, 2014).

Finding My Activist Voice by April Yamasaki

12   Deborah Koehn Loyd, *Your Vocational Credo: Practical Steps to Discover Your Unique Purpose* (Downers Grove, IL: InterVarsity Press, 2015).

13   Ibid., 178–82.

14   Ibid., 138.

The Story of a Voice by Linda MacKillop

15   C. S. Lewis, *The Horse and His Boy* (New York: HarperCollins, 1994), 216.

All content for Everbloom *was provided by Members of Redbud Writers Guild, a nonprofit Christian organization committed to expanding the feminine voice.*

Redbud Writers

DR. AMY DAVIS ABDALLAH loves walking the journey of authentic Christian life with others. She takes special interest in the development and needs of women of any ethnicity, age, vocation, or status. Her first book is *The Book of Womanhood* (Cascade, 2015). Amy passionately fulfills the roles of professor, wife, writer, speaker, mentor, mother, and whatever else life presents. In her free time, she enjoys exercise, photography, climbing mountains, travel, adventuring with her husband and son, learning languages, and the creative arts. Follow her on Twitter @amyfdavisa and on Facebook at amyfdavisabdallah; amyfdavisabdallah.com.

LINDSEY W. ANDREWS is an attorney, writer, blogger, and social media maven. She is tolerated by two adopted kids and a husband, but is adored by a French bulldog, Walter. Her work has been featured across the Internet, and she has self-published a children's book series about global social justice issues. See her writing about finding joy in online business, travel, people, and food at lindseyandrewswriter.com.

JENNY RAE ARMSTRONG is passionate about building up the body of Christ by building up women. A pastor at Darrow Road Wesleyan Church and member of Redbud's board of directors, her work has appeared in dozens of publications including *Relevant*, *Her.meneutics*, and *Red Letter Christians*, and her articles on gender justice and empowering women and girls have won multiple awards from the Evangelical Press Association and the Associated Church

Press. She is the author of *Don't Hide Your Light under a Laundry Basket: 150 Bright Ideas for Wannabe World Changers,* and Christians for Biblical Equality's international youth curriculum, *Called Out.* Jenny has a BA in global studies from University of Northwestern, and is pursuing an MDiv at North Park Theological Seminary. Connect with her at jennyraearmstrong.com.

SUZANNE BURDEN is a pastor, writer, and speaker who communicates about life in the kingdom of God as a joyful, right-now reality. Her bumpy journey through disability, depression, seminary, and childlessness—combined with her education in communications and theology—offers authentic hope for those seeking to realize their place and value. She enjoys preaching at her church and teaching at retreats, conferences, and university chapels, and her writing has appeared in publications including The Junia Project blog, *SheLoves Magazine*, and *Christianity Today*. She also coauthored the book *Reclaiming Eve: The Identity and Calling of Women in the Kingdom of God* and the Reclaiming Eve Small Group DVD. Suzanne and her husband, David, live in Fort Wayne, Indiana, where they share a fondness for his cooking skills. Find out more at suzanneburden.com.

With grace and humor, HEATHER CREEKMORE writes and speaks hope to a woman's struggle with comparison and body image. She hails from Dallas, Texas, where she lives with her husband, Eric, a pastor and church planter, and four children. Heather connects with women weekly through speaking and her blog, *Compared to Who?* Her first book, with the same title, releases June 2017 (visit comparedtowho.me).

LESLIE LEYLAND FIELDS is the multi-award winning author of ten books, including *Forgiving Our Fathers and Mothers, The Spirit of Food,* and *Surviving the Island of Grace.* Her most recent, *Crossing the Waters: Following Jesus through the Storms, the Fish, the Doubt, and the Seas* won the 2017 CT Book Award for Christian Living. Leslie lives on Kodiak Island, Alaska, where she leads the Harvester Island Wilderness Workshop for writers, and where she works in commercial fishing with her husband and six (mostly grown) children. She blogs about her Alaskan life, adventures, and travels at leslieleylandfields.com.

SARAH FINCH is a writer and aspiring author whose passion is to fulfill her calling in the chaos of life. Her focus right now is discipling her two young children and a group of senior girls she's had the privilege of walking with since middle school. A storyteller at heart, she is passionate about weaving beautiful tales from seemingly mundane moments. Lifelong goals include getting an MFA, running a marathon, writing a book, and seeing her children know Jesus. Connect with her on Facebook, Twitter, and Instagram @sebstuff; sarahelizabethfinch.com.

After the early death of her mother, ADELLE GABRIELSON spent years feeling discontented—years struggling with worry, fear, doubt, and a daily sense of failure. Through a journey of personal discovery, loss, grief, and God's gentle guidance, Adelle has come to find freedom in her flaws. Her writing can be found in publications from LifeWay, DaySpring, and Focus on the Family. Adelle lives in New Hampshire with her husband and two sons, and blogs at adellegabrielson.com.

EMILY GIBSON is a wife, mother, farmer, and family physician, living the rural life in northwest Washington State. She chronicles life on the farm on her blog, *Barnstorming*, with daily harvesting stories, essays, poetry, and photography, some of which have been reposted on Ann Voskamp's Only the Good Stuff at aholyexperience.com. In addition, her medical opinion pieces have appeared on kevinmd.com and *Her.meneutics.* Several dozen stories have been published in *Country* magazine and her writing is featured in two anthologies, *Between Midnight and Dawn* edited by Sarah Arthur and *The Jane Effect: Celebrating Jane Goodall.* Learn more at briarcroft.wordpress.com.

DOROTHY GRECO spends her days working as a writer, photographer, journalist, and pastor. She is passionate about leading others in reconciliation and transformation. Dorothy is a featured contributor for *CT Women*, *Gifted for Leadership*, and *Start Marriage Right.* Represented by Credo, Dorothy's first book, *Making Marriage Beautiful*, will be published by David C. Cook in January 2017. Find more of her work at dorothygreco.com.

A cross-cultural missionary, ILONA K. HADINGER has lived in Mexico with her family for the past eighteen years. A polyglot, she speaks English, Spanish, and Hungarian (her first language), and has studied Plautdietsch. Her articles have appeared in *Gifted for Leadership*, *Tortilla Press* (LAC [Latin America and Caribbean] Writers Guild), Cleveland.com, and *Thrive Connection.* An award-winning photographer, she brings both calling and creativity together at ikhadinger.com.

ASHLEY HALES is a writer, speaker, busy mom of four, and wife to a church planter in Southern California. She holds a PhD in English from the University of Edinburgh in Scotland, but she spends most of her time chasing around her children and helping her husband plant a church. Her writing has appeared in *Books & Culture*, *Think Christian*, *Englewood Review of Books*, The Gospel Coalition, *The Well*, and *(in)courage,* among other places. She is writing a book, provisionally titled *Finding Holy in the Suburbs*, forthcoming from InterVarsity Press.

Follow Ashley on social media at @aahales, at *The Mudroom* (where she edits and writes monthly), and on her website, aahales.com.

SHARON R. HOOVER is a speaker, author, and traveler. She serves as the director of missions at Centreville Presbyterian Church and is on the Redbud board of directors. Her first book, *Soul Motive to Pray*, is a personal retreat workbook to encourage deeper conversations with God. Sharon writes regularly for print and digital publications on missions, discipleship, and living a faith-filled journey. She lives in Virginia with her husband and occasionally visiting young adult children. Connect with her at sharonrhoover.com.

TARYN HUTCHISON has lived in three countries and visited a host of others on six continents. She wrote her first book, *We Wait You: Waiting on God in Eastern Europe*, after a career as a single missionary, and has published a few short stories and articles—winning an Amy Writing Award for one of those. Taryn spent her childhood in a town of seventy-five people, three million chickens, and two imaginary friends. Recently, she's come full circle to live in a sleepy town where she works at the small university where she obtained her master of arts in writing. Learn more at tarynhutchison.com.

After kicking around with a Moleskine for years and thinking *The New Yorker* was the only place to publish, KATHERINE JAMES finally decided to get her MFA. At Columbia University she received the Felipe P. De Alba fellowship and taught fiction. She went on to study at Bread Loaf Writers' Conference. As well as being published in various journals and anthologies, her novel *Can You See Anything Now* was a semifinalist for the Bakwin Award, and one of her short stories was a finalist for a *Narrative* Spring Story Prize. She has a novel, as well as a memoir recounting the story of her son's overdose on heroin, forthcoming from Paraclete Press. Katherine and her husband, Rick, have been blessed to work with the ministry of Cru for twenty-nine years and continue to be amazed at how God draws people to himself. She blogs at northhillsdrive.com.

ALIA JOY is the daughter of both a book lover and a storyteller and in that she was destined to be a writer. She is also a collector of words, a speaker, and a homeschooling mother of three making her home in Central Oregon with her husband, Josh, her mother, a bunny, and a bunch of chickens. She shares her life with readers of her blog—aliajoy.com—weaving beauty throughout even the most broken of stories. Her work touches on so many of the hurts of today's women—depression and abuse, race and culture, body image and the hard work of seeing God's glory in the mess. Alia's unique perspective and raw vulnerability make her an approachable voice, a place to come and say, "me, too." She is also a regular monthly contributor at *(in)courage*, *SheLoves Magazine*, *GraceTable*, *The Mudroom*, and Deeper Waters. Find her on Twitter @AliaJoyH where she'll be hashtagging all the things and drinking copious amounts of coffee. Learn more at http://aliajoy.com.

TERRI KRAUS has authored or coauthored thirteen novels—both historical and contemporary—adding her award-winning interior designer's eye to her world of fiction. Terri enjoys volunteering on the design team at The Re:new Project (a ministry to refugee women), leading a neighborhood Bible study, Italian cooking, international travel, and all things British. Her book club is in its nineteenth year of meeting monthly. She is the founder of the West Chicagoland Anti-Trafficking Coalition and president of the Redbud Writers Guild. Terri makes her home in Wheaton, Illinois, with her husband, Jim (now empty nesters with son, Elliot, at Taylor University), their miniature schnauzer, Sadie, and Siberian cat, Petey. Connect with her at terrikraus.com.

LARA KRUPICKA is an internationally published parenting journalist, essayist, and author. She is best known for her Bucket List Life Manifesto and her books, *Family Bucket Lists* and *Bucket List Living for Moms*. Lara serves on the executive board of the Redbud Writers Guild as treasurer. When she's not writing, she loves crafting and playing board games with her family. Lara and her husband, Mike, are raising their three daughters in the western suburbs of Chicago.

BRONWYN LEA is a writer, international conference speaker, and lover of conversations over coffee. Born in South Africa, she now lives in California with her husband and three littles. She is passionate that people should know they are deeply loved by God and that their lives are eternally significant. Bronwyn writes at various fun places around the web, including *Christianity Today*'s *Her.meneutics*, *Relevant*, *The Huffington Post*, and *Scary Mommy*. She blogs weekly about all things holy and hilarious at bronlea.com. Find her on Twitter @bronleatweets and on Facebook; bronlea.com.

LINDA MACKILLOP writes fiction and creative nonfiction and works in publishing. Her creative nonfiction has appeared in *Relief Journal* and other literary journals. She is the author of an adult novel, *Try Again Farm,* and a novel for middle school readers, *Hotel, Oscar, Mike, Echo.* Linda earned her BS in communications from Florida State University and her MFA in creative writing from the Rainier Writers Workshop. She and her husband, Bill, are the parents of four grown sons. Linda blogs at opsimathjourney.blogspot.com.

ALEAH MARSDEN is a board member of Redbud Writers Guild and serves as its social media director. Her work can be found in publications like *Christianity Today* and *Books & Culture*; she also wrote a handful of devotionals in the *NIV Bible for Women: Fresh Insights for Thriving in Today's World* (Zondervan, 2015). She has spoken at numerous women's events, moms' groups, and retreats. Aleah also does communications work for Living Bread Ministries. Connect with her on Twitter and Instagram @aleahmarsden, Facebook at aleahnmarsden, or her website at aleahmarsden.com.

CATHERINE MCNIEL is a seeker who writes to open eyes to the creative and redemptive work of God in each moment. She is the author of *Long Days of Small Things: Motherhood as a Spiritual Discipline* (NavPress, 2017), and her writing has been published in numerous books and articles. Catherine serves alongside her husband in a community-based ministry, while caring for three kids, two jobs, and one enormous garden. Connect with Catherine at catherinemcniel.com or on Twitter @catherinemcniel.

CARA MEREDITH is a writer and speaker from Seattle, Washington. She is cohost of the monthly Shalom Book Club podcast, and a regular contributor to *Gifted for Leadership*, *SheLoves Magazine* and *The Mudroom*. Cara reviews books for *Books & Culture*, *Englewood Review of Books*, and *The Christian Century*, among others. A former high school English teacher, Cara was in full-time ministry before getting an MA in theology from Fuller Seminary. Connect with her at carameredith.com, on Twitter @caramac54, and on Facebook.

JEN POLLOCK MICHEL is the award-winning author of *Teach Us to Want* and *Keeping Place*. She writes widely for print and digital publications and travels to speak at churches, conferences, and retreats. Jen holds a BA in French from Wheaton College and an MA in literature from Northwestern University. She is married to Ryan and together they have five school-age children and live in Toronto. Find more at jenpollockmichel.com or follow Jen on Twitter @jenpmichel.

PEGGY MINDREBO embraces her calling to "bloom where she is planted." Wistful Vista Farm is her home and the place where work, play, and worship intersect. She is a spiritual director and can be found riding horses, paddleboarding, or just walking around her property with those whom she meets. Serving as a pastor at her church gives her many opportunities to speak and teach.

SHAYNE MOORE is the founder of Redbud Writers Guild and editor-in-chief at *The Redbud Post*. Her book *Refuse to Do Nothing: Finding Your Power to Abolish Modern Day Slavery* (InterVarsity Press) was honored as a 2014 Resource of the Year by *Outreach* magazine. Her first book, *Global Soccer Mom: Changing the World Is Easier Than You Think* (Zondervan), chronicles her work with the HIV/AIDS pandemic and received an endorsement from rock singer Bono. With an MA in theology and varied interests, Shayne is a freelance writer for nonprofit organizations and is currently in the Professional Program in Screenwriting at UCLA's School of Theater, Film and Television.

JANNA NORTHRUP loves to write about heartfelt issues of soul care and self-care. She has worked in ministry for most of her adult life as both a youth pastor and Bible study teacher. She has written for *Get Healthy U* and a small local hometown magazine, and is currently writing a memoir. You can follow her on Twitter @ jjnorthr.

NILWONA NOWLIN is a redemptive artist, someone who believes in the power of the arts to bring about positive transformation in individuals and communities. Recent work includes "To Save Many Lives: Exploring Reconciliation Between Africans and African Americans through the Selling of Joseph" for *The Covenant Quarterly* and devotions for *The Covenant Home Altar*. She has presented workshops and facilitated discussions on topics including leadership development, racial reconciliation, and the gift of introversion. Nilwona earned a BA from Columbia College Chicago, an MA in Christian formation and Certificate in justice ministry from North Park Theological Seminary, and a master of nonprofit administration degree from North Park University. Nilwona serves on the Redbud Writers Guild Spiritual Formation Committee and is a member of the ministerial leadership team of Kingdom Covenant Church in Chicago. She blogs at *The Dreamer Speaks*. Follow her on Twitter @nilwona; thedreamerspeaks.com.

R U T H B E L L O L S S O N is an activist at heart. After more than a decade of HIV/AIDS advocacy, Ruth's channels of activism now focus on the systemic issues that surround and compound the pandemic. These include gender inequality and patriarchy, LGBTQ inclusion, nonviolence and peacemaking, as well as changing the world's approach to the global orphan crisis. Ruth earned her bachelor of arts degree in philosophy from Wheaton College and her master of arts degree in global leadership from Fuller Seminary. Ruth has traveled to some of the hardest places in the world and has witnessed God in every corner. She writes and speaks on a variety of subjects and loves to wrestle with the deep mysteries of living a life of faith in a complicated world. Ruth and her husband, Jeff, are founding members of Mars Hill Bible Church, and they live in Grand Rapids with their three children: Zinnia, Oskar, and Kagiso.

T A M M Y P E R L M U T T E R writes about unabridged life, fragmented faith, and investing in the mess of it all, and is the founder and curator of the collaborative blog *The Mudroom*. She cofounded Deeply Rooted, a biannual worship event for women. Tammy lives in intentional community with Jesus People USA in Chicago. She has an essay in the *Soul Bare* anthology (InterVarsity Press). Learn more at tammygrrrl.com.

MARGARET ANN PHILBRICK is an author, gardener, and teacher who desires to plant seeds in hearts. Her debut novel, *A Minor: A Novel of Love, Music and Memory* (Koehler Books, 2014), explores music and dementia. She created the holiday gift book *Back to the Manger* (Singing River Publications, 2009) with her mother, an oil painter, and her poetry has been published in several anthologies. Margaret serves on the boards of her local church and the Redbud Writers Guild. She is featured in a new video Bible curriculum for the book *Messy Grace* by Pastor Caleb Kaltenbach, aimed at sharing God's love with the LGBT community. Connect with her at margaretphilbrick.com.

TRINA POCKETT is an inspirational speaker, writer, and leader with over fifteen years' experience serving in nonprofit leadership. Trina's own story about her battle with cancer reminds her that life is a gift from God. Through storytelling, humor, and encouragement, Trina shares the incredible adventure of living a life of faith. Trina released her first book, *Unexpected: Grit, Grace and Life In Between*. She is a member of the Redbud Writers Guild, and her work has been featured in numerous magazines including *FullFill* and *Intersections*, and on the MOPS website. Connect with Trina at trinapockett.com or on Twitter @trinapockett.

JOHANNAH REARDON is the senior editor of *The Redbud Post*. She is also a regular contributor to *Gifted for Leadership* and managed *Christianity Today*'s Bible study site for eight years. She has written content for the *Couples' Devotional Bible* and the *Everyday Matters Bible for Women*. In addition to numerous novels, she has written a bestselling family devotional guide called *Proverbs for Kids*. Her latest book, *No More Fear*, is a forty-day devotional on overcoming fear and worry. Learn more at johannahreardon.com.

MALLORY REDMOND is a writer, speaker, and big-time coffee drinker. She received her MA in theology and culture from the Seattle School of Theology & Psychology before moving to Ohio with her husband, Darren, and their pup, Roger. She spends most of her time traveling around the web writing about grace, relationships, faith, grief, and chocolate, among other rich topics, with weekly stories on her blog and at some of the sweetest places online, such as *iBelieve, The Mudroom, Red Tent Living,* and *(in)courage.* Follow her writing, facepalm moments, and endless photos of Roger on both Facebook at mallorylarsenredmond and Twitter @malloryjredmond; malloryredmond.com.

SARAH RENNICKE loves words. She also loves people. And she loves weaving them together in honest and vulnerable ways that cut underneath the surface and break open the longings of the heart. She is a writer and dreamer whose words breathe vulnerability and hope into longing souls. She enjoys slowing down and listening to the heartbeats of this world, and believes that we are all desiring to be seen, known, and loved. Sarah writes for an international sports ministry, has a weekly column at *ALTARWORK*, and invites readers to sit with her awhile at *Dreaming to Stay Awake.* Connect with her on Instagram and Twitter @SRennAwake; sarahrennicke.com.

RONNE ROCK's heart finds its strongest beat where beauty and pain collide—it's there she finds stories that change stories. There's more than thirty years of marketing and communications leadership in her bones, and she shares wisdom as a regular contributor for *Orange.* These days, you'll often find her with the vulnerable in difficult places around the world, gathering stories for Orphan Outreach, and writing as an advocacy journalist for organizations like Food for the Hungry and Compassion International. She's also a blogger, speaker, and aspiring author with a heart for redemption—

her work has appeared in *The Huffington Post, Fiftiness, The Redbud Post, The Good Men Project, The Mudroom, Bedlam Magazine, The Phoenix Soul*, and more. You'll find her personal writings and a little bit of #kitchentherapy at ronnerock.com.

ANGIE RYG is an international speaker who encourages women to find joy in the little things, their beauty and identity in Christ. As a Bible teacher and storyteller, she helps women go deeper into Scripture and apply God's amazing story of grace in everyday moments. She loves to connect with women at MOPS gatherings, conferences, retreats, and around her farm table with some chips and salsa. She is the author of *Clutter Free Simplicity*, and her writing can be found in places including *Her.meneutics, Unlocking the Bible, (in)courage, Whatever Girls,* and Deeper Waters. Married to her childhood sweetheart and mama to one princess and three princes, Angie desires to create a life where laughter and love coexist with her many loads of laundry. Connect with her on Facebook, Twitter, and Instagram @angieryg; angieryg.com.

WHITNEY R. SIMPSON is the author of *Holy Listening with Breath, Body, and the Spirit* from Upper Room Books, a book of meditations inviting you to use your whole self to listen for God. As a survivor of a stroke, brain surgery, and cancer—all before the age of thirty-one—she seeks to experience and share the gifts of God's peace no matter the circumstances. Whitney pursued professional certification in spiritual formation from Garrett-Evangelical Theological Seminary and serves as a retreat facilitator, spiritual director, and yoga instructor. Connect with Whitney via social media at @WhitRSimpson and at exploringpeace.com.

MARGOT STARBUCK, speaker and award-winning author, is passionate about communicating to individuals that they have been made for life that really is life. A graduate of Westmont College and

Princeton Theological Seminary, Margot is the author of *The Girl in the Orange Dress*, *Unsqueezed*, and *Small Things with Great Love*. She lives in Durham, North Carolina, with her husband and three children by birth and adoption. She serves as a volunteer among friends with and without disabilities through Reality Ministries. Convinced that God is with us and for us, in the person of Jesus, Margot inspires audiences to live love in the world. Learn more about Margot's literary consulting at wordmelon.com, and connect at margotstarbuck.com.

NICOLE T. WALTERS is a writer, wife, and working mom from Metro Atlanta, Georgia. She is an editor at *SheLoves Magazine* and *The Mudroom*, and her work has appeared online and in print at places like *Relevant*, *Her.meneutics*, *Ready*, and *Ruminate*. She writes about faith and culture at *A Voice in the Noise* (nicoletwalters.com). Nicole loves to experience and write about the messy, noisy, beautiful world and cultures not her own, and travels internationally as often as she gets the chance. You can follow Nicole on Twitter @NicoleTWalters and Facebook at nicoletwalters.writer; nicoletwalters.com.

PEGGYSUE WELLS is a writer, board member, homeschooler, radio cohost, workshop presenter, and mom with seven favorite children. She has published two dozen books, including a couple of bestsellers, an Audie award finalist that came in second to Keith Richards' memoir read by Johnny Depp, and several coauthored projects including a parenting book with June Hunt because PeggySue writes well with others. Her motto is, "How can we make this happen?" Her work has been described as giving voice to women, empowering others to pursue their full potential, and showing students the essentials that make writing doable. PeggySue specializes in equipping parents to provide a nurturing environment for children. The great connector, PeggySue connects people with similar vision and complementary skills. Connect with her at peggysuewells.com.

APRIL YAMASAKI is the lead pastor of a midsize, multi-staffed church, and the author of *Christ Is for Us: A Lenten Study Based on the Revised Common Lectionary*; *Spark: Igniting Your God-Given Creativity*; *Ordinary Time with Jesus; Sacred Pauses: Spiritual Practices for Personal Renewal;* and other books on Christian living. Her main website, *Writing and Other Acts of Faith* (aprilyamasaki.com), features articles on practical spirituality, like finding a healthy rhythm of work and rest, and how to pray on difficult days. Her second website, *When You Work for the Church: The Good, The Bad, and the Ugly, and How We Can All Do Better* (whenyouworkforthechurch.com), focuses on improving employment practices in churches and other Christian organizations. Find her on Twitter @SacredPauses, or on Facebook; aprilyamasaki.com.

ABOUT PARACLETE PRESS

Who We Are

Paraclete Press is a publisher of books, recordings, and DVDs on Christian spirituality. Our publishing represents a full expression of Christian belief and practice—from Catholic to Evangelical, from Protestant to Orthodox.

We are the publishing arm of the Community of Jesus, an ecumenical monastic community in the Benedictine tradition. As such, we are uniquely positioned in the marketplace without connection to a large corporation and with informal relationships to many branches and denominations of faith.

What We Are Doing

PARACLETE PRESS BOOKS | Paraclete publishes books that show the richness and depth of what it means to be Christian. Although Benedictine spirituality is at the heart of all that we do, we publish books that reflect the Christian experience across many cultures, time periods, and houses of worship. We publish books that nourish the vibrant life of the church and its people.

We have several different series, including the best-selling Paraclete Essentials and Paraclete Giants series of classic texts in contemporary English; Voices from the Monastery—men and women monastics writing about living a spiritual life today; award-winning poetry; best-selling gift books for children on the occasions of baptism and first communion; and the Active Prayer Series that brings creativity and liveliness to any life of prayer.

MOUNT TABOR BOOKS | Paraclete's newest series, Mount Tabor Books, focuses on the arts and literature as well as liturgical worship and spirituality, and was created in conjunction with the Mount Tabor Ecumenical Centre for Art and Spirituality in Barga, Italy.

PARACLETE RECORDINGS | From Gregorian chant to contemporary American choral works, our recordings celebrate the best of sacred choral music composed through the centuries that create a space for heaven and earth to intersect. Paraclete Recordings is the record label representing the internationally acclaimed choir Gloriæ Dei Cantores, praised for their "rapt and fathomless spiritual intensity" by *American Record Guide*; the Gloriæ Dei Cantores Schola, specializing in the study and performance of Gregorian chant; and the other instrumental artists of the Arts Empowering Life Foundation.

Paraclete Press is also privileged to be the exclusive North American distributor of the recordings of the Monastic Choir of St. Peter's Abbey in Solesmes, France, long considered to be a leading authority on Gregorian chant.

PARACLETE VIDEO | Our DVDs offer spiritual help, healing, and biblical guidance for a broad range of life issues including grief and loss, marriage, forgiveness, facing death, bullying, addictions, Alzheimer's, and spiritual formation.

Learn more about us at our website:
www.paracletepress.com or phone us
toll-free at 1.800.451.5006

SCAN
TO
READ
MORE

You may also be interested in Literary Guides for the Church Year by Sarah Arthur, a Redbud Writer . . .

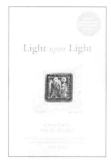

Light upon Light

A Literary Guide to Advent, Christmas and Epiphany

978-1-612-61419-9 $18.99 Paperback

This collection of daily and weekly readings goes through the liturgical seasons of winter—including Advent, Christmas and Epiphany. New voices such as Amit Majmudar and Scott Cairns are paired with well-loved classics by Dickens, Andersen, and Eliot. "In our individual darknesses we long for more light. Sarah Arthur illuminates our whole year with the gift of flaming words. A treasure of enlightenment."

—Luci Shaw, author of *Breath for the Bones* and *Adventure of Ascent*

At the Still Point

A Literary Guide to Prayer in Ordinary Time

978-1-55725-785-7 $16.99 paperback

"What a delight to find so extraordinary a collection meant for use in ordinary time! Any book that includes passages from *The Wind in the Willows* and *Moby Dick*, as well as poems by George Herbert and Christina Rossetti, is all right with me. Especially because each of the works chosen is meant to awaken me to the movement of the spirit in daily life."

—Kathleen Norris, author of *Dakota* and *The Cloister Walk*

Between Midnight and Dawn

A Literary Guide to Prayer for Lent, Holy Week and Eastertide

978-1-61261-663-6 $18.99 Paperback

Experience the liturgical seasons of Lent, Holy Week, and Eastertide in the company of poets and novelists from across the centuries.

Chimamanda Ngozi Adichie and Benjamin Alire Sáenz join well-loved classics by Dostoevsky, Rossetti, and Eliot. Light in the darkness, illuminating the soul. This rich anthology will draw you deeper into God's presence through the medium of the imagination.

Available through your local bookseller or through Paraclete Press:
www.paracletepress.com; 1-800-451-5006

ABOUT THE REDBUD WRITERS GUILD

Redbud Writers Guild is an international community of Christian women who envision a vibrant and diverse movement of women who create in community and who influence culture and faith. Redbud members strive to change the world with words as we foster a safe sisterhood of creatives who thrive in a non-competitive, supportive community.

Interested in membership? Visit our website.

Each month, the women of Redbud publish a free online magazine.
Subscribe today at www.RedbudWritersGuild.com
Follow us on Facebook @redbudwritersguild
and Twitter @redbudwriters